Fugitive Saints

Fugitive Saints

Catholicism and the Politics of Slavery

Katie Walker Grimes

Fortress Press
Minneapolis

FUGITIVE SAINTS

Catholicism and the Politics of Slavery

Cover image: Black Madonna and Child. Haitian/Nicolas Sapieha/Art Resource, NY

Cover design: Laurie Ingram

Print ISBN: 978-1-5064-1672-4

eBook ISBN: 978-1-5064-1673-1

The paper used in this publication meets the minimum requirements of American National Standard for Information Sciences — Permanence of Paper for Printed Library Materials, ANSI Z329.48-1984.

Manufactured in the U.S.A.

This book was produced using Pressbooks.com, and PDF rendering was done by PrinceXML.

Contents

Acknowledgments

I first heard about Peter Claver during graduate school, when a professor mentioned Claver's advocacy for black slaves. After class, I rushed to the campus library to check out every single book I could find about this man. Filled with excitement, I thought, "At last!" I had found the person I had been looking and hoping for: a person who enlisted theological, spiritual, and sacramental resources against black chattel slavery. But, as I turned the pages of some of the very hagiographies discussed in this book, my eager optimism soon turned into confusion and then anger: Peter Claver did not fit the saintly description my professor had ascribed to him. Although I did not find in Claver a racial hero, I could not forget him. I have spent the last several years trying to figure out how a person who treated enslaved people so poorly ended up being remembered as their great champion. The manuscript that follows represents the fruits of that search.

Many people have helped me along the way. I thank James F. Keenan, SJ, for his continued mentorship: Peter Claver made a brief and somewhat tangential appearance in my dissertation, and you were the first to affirm the value of my work on him. My dissertation adviser, M. Shawn Copeland, has also, perhaps unwittingly, helped this project take shape: although I am no longer your student, you are still teaching me. My gratitude extends to my editor, Michael Gibson, who took a chance on this project and has lent his considerable editorial skills to its improvement.

But this manuscript might never have left the inside of my laptop if not for Megan Clark, who gave me much needed encouragement during a time when I lacked confidence. I must also thank Steven Battin, who is one of my favorite conversation partners, for managing simultaneously to affirm and challenge me. I owe so much gratitude to my great friend Sonja Anderson, who always makes time to listen to me and reads any draft I throw her way. My friendship with Michael Jaycox has also sustained me: you continue to accompany me through life even though we live on opposite sides of a very large country.

To my father, Michael Sean Grimes, who told me the best bedtime stories, and to my mother, Mary Anne Frericks Grimes, for reading everything I've ever written and for all of those summertime visits to the Marion Public Library when we were kids. You remain my most important audience. Thank you to my brother, John, and my sister, Kelly, for a lifetime of friendship. And to my wife, Erin, you are the best thing that's ever happened to me.

Preface

This book makes two general claims about the Roman Catholic Church and a more specific one about the intersection of theology and antiblackness: first, the church possesses a truly corporate moral character; second, Catholic sainthood offers a particularly effective way to uncover it; and third, each of these assertions proves especially true with respect to the church's underappreciated participation in black chattel slavery and its ongoing Pan-American afterlife. Africanized slavery pervaded all of the Americas, from Canada to Chile; and although black slavery has been abolished in each of these countries, the racialized world it set in motion has yet to end. What I term antiblackness supremacy—the power nonblack people amass at the expense of black women, children, and men—persists as more than just a memory; it operates as a living, breathing legacy.[1] The claim that the church possesses a corporate body not just metaphorically but also in reality may at first appear rhetorically excessive. But for Catholics, as for other Christians, the ecclesial body of Christ is just as real, and therefore just as historically visible, as any individual human body.[2] Indeed, Christians become the corporate body of Christ every time they performatively receive his body in the Eucharist.[3]

So Catholics frequently speak about the church as though it enacts

1. Saidiya V. Hartman, *Lose Your Mother: A Journey along the Atlantic Slave Route* (New York: Farrar, Straus & Giroux, 2008), 6.
2. M. Shawn Copeland, "The New Anthropological Subject at the Heart of the Mystical Body of Christ," *Proceedings of the Catholic Theological Society of America* 53 (2013).
3. M. Shawn Copeland, *Enfleshing Freedom: Body, Race, and Being* (Minneapolis: Fortress, 2009).

a truly corporate body. Papal encyclicals and pastoral letters offer counsel not just to individual Christians or "men of good will" but also to the church as a corporate body; they describe how the church has acted in the past in order to instruct it how to act in the future. In response, Catholics implicitly credit the church with corporate virtues. But if the church's corporate body enacts virtues, then can it not also succumb to corporate vices? The church's corporate body possesses at least as much reality in its historically visible vices as it does in its virtues. This claim admittedly rubs up against perceptions of ecclesial purity and sinlessness. But while God may preserve an unpolluted space somewhere within the church, the church's actions have left a mark on history that cannot be denied.

Catholic sainthood proves particularly adept at documenting the church's corporate moral character, precisely because it emerges as a product of the church's corporate body. Especially since the Council of Trent, canonization processes have passed through official institutional channels. They also typically require relatively intense and prolonged formal support from religious orders and/or organized laypeople in order to attain success. More than simply expressing how the church processes holiness, canonization campaigns also reveal how power operates in and through the church.

Sainthood also carries corporate memories within it. Official processes of canonization as well as more informally produced hagiographies serve as a popular and deeply rooted form of ecclesial autobiography.[4] In this way, for example, opponents of the recent canonization of the eighteenth-century Spanish missionary Junípero Serra claim that his sainthood falsely portrays the church not as a collaborator in the oppression of indigenous people but as their savior. For them, Serra's sainthood evidences that the church's memory does not always match its lived history. More than simply revealing how the church remembers itself to have acted, sainthood can unveil how the church in fact did act.[5] For these reasons, it enables the church

---

4. Elizabeth A. Johnson, *Friends of God and Prophets: A Feminist Theological Reading of the Communion of Saints* (New York: Continuum, 1998), 10, 27.

to examine its corporate conscience and reconsider its corporate character.

The gap between corporate memory and corporate history proves particularly large with respect to the church's corporate participation in what I term antiblackness supremacy. Although Pope John Paul II apologized to Africans for the church's participation in the slave trade, the church has yet to fully grasp the extent of the church's alliance with it.[6] Much less has the church uncovered the ways in which antiblackness supremacy continues to inhabit its corporate body. The sainthoods of Peter Claver and Martín de Porres, because they are the only Catholics who have been canonized primarily due to their relation to the black chattel slavery that structured life in the Americas for nearly five hundred years, sheds a particularly clear light on the church's relation to antiblackness supremacy. These saints tell a story we ignore at our own peril.

5. Lawrence S. Cunningham, "Saints and Martyrs: Some Contemporary Considerations," *Theological Studies* 60, no. 3 (1999): 529–30.
6. E. J. Dionne Jr., "Pope Apologizes to Africans for Slavery," *New York Times*, August 14, 1985.

Introduction

Despite the fact that black slavery structured life in the Americas for centuries, the church has canonized only two people—the freeborn Peruvian mulatto Martín de Porres and the Spanish born Jesuit Peter Claver—whose lives are connected to this evil practice. Through these men, I argue, the church remembers itself as a hero to black slaves and their racialized descendants. In the decades after abolition, for example, white Catholics in the United States began to exalt both Claver as "the apostle of the Negroes" and Porres as the patron saint of mixed-race people and racial harmony.[1]

But in truth neither man deemed Africanized slavery to be evil; nor apparently has the church: it has not considered opposition to black slavery either a sign of holiness or a requirement for it. Even worse, both Claver and Porres appeared extraordinarily holy to their earliest advocates not because they challenged or destabilized the regnant racial order but precisely for the ways they held it together. Rather than protecting black slaves from slavery as his champions claim, Claver instead helped to incorporate them into it. And rather than using Christian humility in order to subvert the racial order, Porres enacted a racially bifurcated version of it.[2] Both sainthoods also helped to fashion and justify a distinctly Catholic theology of Africanized

---

1. John Richard Slattery, *The Life of St. Peter Claver, S.J.: The Apostle of the Negroes* (Philadelphia: Kilner, 1893).
2. For examples of this hagiographical trope, see Alex García-Rivera, *St. Martín de Porres: The "Little Stories" and the Semiotics of Culture* (Maryknoll, NY: Orbis, 1995).

slavery in which re-fashioned supposedly racially neutral Catholic virtues such as humility, love, respect for authority, and peace accorded with the logic of racialized slavery.[3] Catholics endorsed Africanized slavery not *despite* their Catholic habituation but largely *because* of it.

Defining Racial Evil

The church overestimates its corporate racial virtue because it misunderstands racial evil. Today, we inhabit not the aftermath of slavery but its afterlife. The afterlife of slavery attempts to preserve, revivify, and reinvent the association between blackness and slave status, both materially and symbolically, by whatever means necessary.[4] But what is slavery? Slavery does more than simply force people to labor for free or reduce them to property.[5] As Orlando Patterson explains, slavery comprises "the permanent, violent domination of natally alienated and generally dishonored persons."[6] As such, it plunges its victims into a state of social death and operates as the "ultimate form of parasitism."[7] Slavery also justifies itself by figuring enslaved people as those who deserved to die, due either to criminal misconduct or defeat on the battlefield, but were allowed to live due to a stranger's mercy. Given a gift he does not deserve and owing his master a debt he can never repay, an enslaved person is expected to feel only gratitude toward his captor.

Because slavery enacts a unique form of power, so does its ongoing afterlife. Each of slavery's components still presses down on black people even today. More than simply harming black people, the afterlife of slavery empowers everyone else: nonblacks feed off of both black people and blackness much as individual masters did. I therefore

---

3. Second Vatican Council, *Constitution on the Church = Lumen Gentium* (Washington, DC: National Catholic Welfare Conference, 1964), pars. 40, 50.
4. Hortense J. Spillers, "Mama's Baby, Papa's Maybe: An American Grammar Book," in *Black, White, and in Color: Essays on American Literature and Culture* (Chicago: University of Chicago Press, 2003), 207–8.
5. Orlando Patterson, *Slavery and Social Death: A Comparative Study* (Cambridge, MA: Harvard University Press, 1985), 17–18, 27–28,
6. Ibid., 14.
7. Ibid., 334–42.

designate this form of racial evil by the term "antiblackness supremacy" in order to identify the fact that all nonblack people, especially white ones, amass both power and privilege at black people's expense.

Why call this form of supremacy "antiblackness supremacy?" The phrase "antiblackness supremacy" undoubtedly sounds syntactically wooden. But, rather than being a weakness, such awkwardness represents a strength. Precisely because it does not roll easily off the tongue, "antiblackness supremacy" operates in interruptive fashion; it cannot be aesthetically assimilated. Unlike the phenomenon of antiblackness supremacy, whose routine pervasiveness, like camouflage, can make it appear not to exist at all, the phrase "antiblackness supremacy" cannot be rendered ordinary, mundane, or familiar.[8] It sticks out precisely because it does not fit within sentences the way that we expect it to.[9] And in contrast to other popular racial terms such as "white supremacy" or "white privilege," the term "antiblackness supremacy" explicitly positions black people as victimized by the unique form of power unleashed by the Africanization of slavery.

And in contrast to the term "antiblack," the term antiblackness supremacy neutralizes what I identify as the "What about Oprah?" defense. This defense points to the economic prosperity, power, and acclaim enjoyed by prominent black individuals such as Oprah Winfrey, Barack Obama, and Michael Jordan as evidence that racial injustice no longer prevails.[10] The noun *antiblackness* creates more rhetorical and conceptual space to consider the ways in which racial evil operates as a corporate act. It also better captures the dynamic

8. Saidiya V. Hartman, *Scenes of Subjection: Terror, Slavery, and Self-Making in Nineteenth-Century America* (New York: Oxford University Press, 1997), 3, 4.

9. For more on the rationale behind this term, see my chapter titled "Black Exceptionalism: Antiblackness Supremacy in the Afterlife of Slavery," in a forthcoming book on antiblackness edited by Vincent Lloyd and Andrew Prevot.

10. For recent examples of the "What about Oprah?" defense, see Mark Joseph, "No, Oprah, America Isn't Racist," *USA TODAY*, November 25, 2013, http://tinyurl.com/zu7vfr7; Jonah Goldberg, "Oprah, Obama, and the Racism Dodge," *National Review Online*, November 20, 2013, http://tinyurl.com/pulet76; "O'Reilly Clashes with Harvard Professor over Oprah: She's 'Indicting' America as a Racist Nation," FoxNation.com, November 19, 2013, http://tinyurl.com/zy4x943; Daniel Schorr, "A New, 'Post-Racial' Political Era in America," NPR.org, January 28, 2008, http://tinyurl.com/mypcmr.

character of racial oppression; just as racial boundaries do, so racialized power changes over time, conceding to new pressures and seizing new opportunities.

Catholic Saints and Racial Virtue

More than simply habituated by slavery's ongoing afterlife, Catholic hagiographical processes have helped to animate it. In particular, the sainthoods of Claver and Porres have helped to promote the following: a perverse attachment to black gratitude; an immoderate fear of black rebellion; an uncritical celebration of interracial proximity, affection, and love; an insatiable desire for white saviors and heroes; and a misplaced desire to elevate white heroes. Thus, even when deployed by white Catholic champions of racial justice, their sainthoods only affirmed the racially distorted worldviews of even these well-intentioned whites. They did even less to disrupt the bad racial habits of their more vicious counterparts. Ultimately, while their sainthoods may have helped advance causes such as ecclesial inclusion and social integration, neither that of Claver nor Porres has undermined antiblackness supremacy's root cause, the afterlife of Africanized slavery.

Corporate confidence in these men's racial virtue nonetheless has only grown with time. In recent decades, U.S. Catholics have continued to update the stories of Claver and Porres, refashioning them to fit within the ideological parameters of the post–Civil Rights Era. For example, on its parish website, Saint Peter Claver Church in Los Angeles describes Claver as a racial visionary and emancipator in the style of Abraham Lincoln and Martin Luther King Jr. To this end, it contrasts the "brutal dehumanization [done] by slave masters" with the "self-respect, dignity, and worth" that Claver supposedly conferred on the slaves he encountered. In this same spirit, the Catholic Worker House located on the predominantly black Westside of South Bend, Indiana, bears his name, and popular Jesuit priest James Martin calls Claver "one of my favorite Jesuit saints."[11] And, in his 2000 pastoral letter on racism, Chicago's Cardinal Francis George praised Porres as one of several saints who "has especially promoted racial harmony and social justice."[12]

The subjective adaptability of our hagiographical memory is not in itself bad.[13] Like all saints, Claver and Porres have served as icons of the church's self image and narrate an ecclesial autobiography.[14] But this plasticity has allowed contemporary Catholics to imagine these saints as symbols of not what the church was but what they wish it had been. In misremembering these men, the church also misremembers itself. More than simply perceiving their purported racial virtuousness as evidence of its own, the church celebrates its celebration of them: as one white, twentieth-century cleric proclaimed, "The Church not only baptizes and ordains and consecrates Negroes and mulattoes: She canonizes them as saints."[15] How can the church repent for sins it has not yet acknowledged?

But perhaps the recent canonization of Josephine Bakhita, a Sudanese-born slave who found freedom in Italy, proves that the church has begun to build new hagiographical habits. However, although Bakhita was holy, her sainthood will do little to disrupt the operation of the specific vice of antiblackness supremacy within the church's corporate body. Bakhita's enslavement came at the hands of Arab, predominantly Muslim masters, while American slavery was sustained almost exclusively by white Christians. When the church celebrates the holiness only of those black slaves who have suffered from someone else's cruelty, it indulges in what I identify as Catholic racial triumphalism. This deeply rooted ideology presents the church as the supreme liberator of black slaves and their descendants and denies any participation in or culpability for their enslavement and

11. Alex Mikulich, Laurie Cassidy, and Margaret Pfeil, *The Scandal of White Complicity in US Hyper-incarceration: A Nonviolent Spirituality of White Resistance* (New York: Palgrave Macmillan, 2013), xv; James Martin's Facebook page. Accessed September 9, 2013. http://tinyurl.com/hj2tbqv.

12. See Cardinal Francis George, *Dwell in My Love: A Pastoral Letter on Racism,* April 4, 2001, http://tinyurl.com/jkwhgbk.

13. And certainly, none of the aforementioned Catholics would deny that Claver was flawed, but they believe Claver's ministry to the blacks truly saintly.

14. Michel de Certeau, *The Writing of History* (New York: Columbia University Press, 1988), 272, 280.

15. Celia Langdeau Cussen, *Black Saint of the Americas: The Life and Afterlife of Martín de Porres* (New York: Cambridge University Press, 2014), 194.

continued oppression. In this way, the church enacts the corporate vice of antiblackness supremacy through not just what it imagines but also what it refuses to admit about itself.

What about the pending cause to canonize the Haitian-born former slave Pierre Toussaint? Unlike Bakhita, he was held by white Catholic masters. Surely his canonization campaign evidences at least some racial progress. However, despite initial appearances, the story of Toussaint's holiness in fact perpetuates a racialized ideology of white mastership and black servility perhaps even more emphatically than the sainthoods of Claver and Porres do. It does so not because Toussaint was not holy but because the church's racial vices are tenacious. Indeed, unlike these other men's sainthoods processes, Toussaint's was not initiated until 1951, nearly a full century after slavery's abolition. Toussaint's case proves that the church cannot build new hagiographical habits simply by canonizing black Catholics, even those who endured slavery. The church cannot simply move beyond its bad racial habits; it must deliberately unmake them.

Of course the church needs more black Catholic saints, just as unacknowledged black Catholic saints deserve to be recognized as such. But the church does not corporately enact antiblackness supremacy because it has failed to canonize a sufficient number of black Catholic saints; the church has failed to canonize a sufficient number of black Catholic saints because it continues corporately to enact the vice of antiblackness supremacy.[16] As long as the church retains its antiblack habits, it will continue to struggle to describe black holiness in a way that does not affirm the logic of slavery's afterlife. One cannot expect to find something one cannot recognize simply by searching for it harder.

16. For more on the truly corporate character of the body of Christ, see Bernard P. Prusak, "Theological Considerations—Hermeneutical, Ecclesiological, and Eschatological Regarding," in *Memory and Reconciliation: The Church and the Faults of the Past" Horizons* 32, no. 1 (April 2005), 140–41.

Fugitive Saints

How, then, can the church begin to build new hagiographical habits? Inspired by the insights of a group of scholars sometimes known as "Afro-pessimists," this project offers black *fugitivity* as a strategy of corporate rehabituation.[17] Why? Although slavery consisted of more than simply preventing enslaved people from running away, it cannot inflict its other harms—natal alienation, social death, dishonor, and spectacular violence to name a few—unless it keeps enslaved people in their place. For this reason, black fugitives defied white mastership not just when they took flight, but also when they moved to spaces that were inaccessible to white supervision or in ways that were unsanctioned by white power. Still today antiblackness supremacy strives to place black people under surveillance in order to keep them under spatial control.[18] During the afterlife of slavery, black people continue to enact fugitivity any time they are perceived to be out of place, whether physically or metaphorically.

The concept of black fugitivity also enhances our understanding of the church's racial guilt. Just as the afterlife of slavery structures the world, so it pervades the church. Metabolizing the fruits of this racist habitat, the church participates in antiblackness supremacy in distinctly Catholic fashion. The sainthoods of Claver, Porres, and Toussaint in particular all have prevented black people from enacting fugitivity both during their lives and through the church's memory of them. In addition to occasionally recapturing runaway slaves or voluntarily submitting to enslavement themselves, these men also have helped to portray black fugitivity as sinful. The church has

17. While these scholars do not necessarily all embrace this term, the designation "Afro-pessimism" is often used to refer to the work of scholars like Fred Moten, Jared Sexton, Frank Wilderson, and Saidiya Hartman, who enlist Orlando Patterson's definition of slavery as social death to argue that black social life in the United States unfolds within what Hartman terms "the afterlife of slavery." These scholars also tend to draw heavily from the work of Frantz Fanon. For more on the debate surrounding this term, see Jared Sexton, "Afro-Pessimism: The Unclear Word," *Rhizomes: Cultural Studies in Emerging Knowledge*, no. 29 (2016), http://tinyurl.com/joxt76z.
18. Neil Roberts, *Freedom as Marronage: The Dialectic of Slavery and Freedom in Arendt, Pettit, Rousseau, Douglass, and the Haitian Revolution* (Phd diss., The University of Chicago, 2007), 2.

opposed black fugitivity for specifically Catholic reasons and in specifically Catholic ways.

Their sainthoods further fuel the church's racially vicious habituation by discouraging the church from the deploying a fugitive approach to its hagiographical history. What do I mean by this? Catholics have updated the memories of Claver, Porres, and Toussaint alike primarily in support of the changing racial aspirations of successive generations of predominantly white Catholic racial reformers. Rather than distancing the church from its habits of racialized mastership, they end up strengthening them. In expanding the margins of the past that the church remembers as its own in this way, the church refuses the fugitivity of those black women and men who both escaped the institutional church and whose memory could not be captured by it.[19] Even well-intentioned white Catholics treat the past as their slave.

Enlisted as hagiographical strategy, fugitivity enables the church to forge a new way of remembering its past. Taking inspiration from actual black fugitives, it instructs the church to listen to the repressed and excluded voices of the racial prophets of the past without claiming them as its own. A fugitive approach to Catholic sainthood proposes the following: rather than seeking retroactively to place its saints on the side of racial justice, the church ought to permit the dangerous memories of the racially righteous to remain outside of it, undomesticated and fugitive. The church ought to judge all candidates for racial holiness by their relation to black fugitivity. A person does not bring racial "good news" unless she makes black fugitivity, as both a historical practice and an interpretive principle, more possible, not less so.

This prescription for a fugitive approach to the church's hagiographical memory neither disregards nor devalues other forms of resistance and survival. Black people have resisted antiblackness supremacy in many other ways—procuring abortions; committing suicide; poisoning their masters; slyly manipulating and/or outwitting

19. Fred Moten, "The Case of Blackness," *Criticism* 50, no. 2 (2008): 179.

them; falling in love; making music, poetry, and art; remaining behind in order to care for a child or an aging elder—to name just a few.[20] This book singles out fugitivity for its unique capacity to chasten antiblack habits of perceiving, acting, and doing theology; it does not, however, affirm the holiness of black fugitivity in order to deny the existence of authentic black saints who remained either under their masters' power or within the church's institutional structures.[21] It contends only that the church cannot hope to perceive these forms of holiness clearly until it first learns to appreciate the holiness displayed both in black fugitivity and by actual black fugitives.

Fugitive Memories

Before I present this fugitive approach to hagiography, I first must substantiate what may appear to be a specious claim that the church possesses a corporate character. Since this project primarily considers the church's hagiographical memory and its saint-making processes, the term *church* refers primarily to its historical and institutional existence. For this reason, I do not, for example, include "anonymous" Christians as members of the historically visible, institutional church.[22] Since this book analyzes the church's history through the lens provided by virtue theory, it treats the content of the church's character as the question it seeks to answer rather than the answer it knows in advance.[23] Like all moral agents, the church becomes what it does: we discern the church's identity by tracking its actions in history.[24] While the church receives its identity as a gift of God's grace, it has not always performatively received this identity as it should.[25]

20. Junius P. Rodriguez, *Encyclopedia of Slave Resistance and Rebellion*, vol. 2 (Westport, CT: Greenwood, 2007), 381, 455, 491, 501; Bernard Moitt, *Women and Slavery in the French Antilles, 1635-1848* (Bloomington, IN: Indiana University Press, 2001), 125.
21. See, for example, M. Shawn. Copeland, "A Cadre of Women Religious Committed to Black Liberation: The National Black Sisters' Conference," *U.S. Catholic Historian* 14, no. 1 (1996): 123–44.
22. I do not deny that so-called "anonymous Christians" exist, however. For more on this, see Karl Rahner, "Observations on the Problem of the 'Anonymous' Christian" (*Theological Investigations* 14 [1976]: 280–94). For more on the development of church teaching regarding the salvation of non-Christians, see Francis A. Sullivan, *Salvation Outside the Church?: Tracing the History of the Catholic Response* (Eugene, OR: Wipf and Stock, 1992).
23. Prusak, "Theological Considerations," 143.
24. Thomas Aquinas, *Summa Theologica*, I–II.53.1 ad 1; 53.3; 71.4.

The term *church* therefore also measures the gap between the former and the latter.[26]

Because this project focuses on memory and fugitivity, however, it does use the term *church* in an admittedly idiosyncratic way, but not unjustifiably so. As with individual human beings, the church is, in a real sense, what it can remember of itself. But, also like individual human beings, it is of course more than that. Sometimes, then, the term *church* designates the identity the church has acquired as a result of its memories; in other cases, the term *church* speaks to this more objective identity that exists independently of the church's memories.[27] In this way, while some of American history's models of black fugitivity would have been fugitives from the church in both senses of the term, others would have been fugitives of the church only in the former sense of the term. These women and men would have considered themselves members of the Catholic Church in one way or another. As a hagiographical corrective, black fugitivity does not necessarily indicate that anyone ought to flee their relationship with Christ. It does not even require that one part ways with the institutional church.

More than simply reflecting the corporately vicious character of the church, this terminological duality also results from the nature of fugitivity itself. Just as the church both is and is not what it remembers itself to be, so fugitivity both should and should not exist. It should not exist in the sense that human beings should not be enslaved in the first place. Human beings may rightly wish to construct a future without this form of fugitivity. Since we inhabit slavery's afterlife, however, we have not yet outrun history's captors. For this reason, fugitivity must be preserved as long as slavery and its afterlives endure, because, in ending it, we would block an exit route out of enslavement.

25. Louis-Marie Chauvet, *Symbol and Sacrament: A Sacramental Reinterpretation of Christian Existence* (Collegeville, MN: Liturgical Press, 1995), 146, 407, 425; Louis-Marie Chauvet, *The Sacraments: The Word of God at the Mercy of the Body* (Collegeville, MN: Liturgical Press, 2001), 90, 105.
26. Bradford E. Hinze, "Ecclesial Repentance and the Demands of Dialogue," *Theological Studies* 61, no. 2 (June 200), 209.
27. This distinction parallels the distinction Rahner makes between the "invisible and visible church." O'Donovan et al., "A Changing Ecclesiology in a Changing Church: A Symposium on Development in the Ecclesiology of Karl Rahner," *Theological Studies* 38, no. 4 (1977): 744.

The church's inability to remember the saintliness of those who resisted antiblackness supremacy qualifies as similarly ambiguous. The fact that their lives have escaped and could not be captured by operative mechanisms of ecclesial memory indicts the church as aligned with enslavement and its afterlife, even if these fugitives counted themselves as Catholics. But the fact that these memories became fugitives in the first place means they must be allowed to remain as such, at least for now. The church participates in its own redemption not by seeking to recapture these memories but by recognizing itself as their captor.[28] Paraphrasing M. Shawn Copeland, Candace McLean explains, "There is wisdom and resistance that comes just from remembering what has been utterly lost."[29] The church's racial dysfunction lies not just in the way the church perceives its past but also in the church's past itself.

Rather than reducing the church to its racial vices, this project interrogates the church's hagiographical imagination in order to compel Catholics to stop underestimating those vices.[30] This analysis does not therefore reduce either hagiography or its critique to mere ideology. It instead takes seriously the Second Vatican Council's describing the church as "at the same time holy and always in need of being purified."[31] Why should we expect its processes of sainthood to be exempt from this?[32] While we should not confuse hagiography critique with historical positivism, neither should we shield the

28. Jared Sexton, "The Social Life of Social Death: On Afro-Pessimism and Black Optimism," *Tensions* 5 (Fall–Winter 2011): 10.
29. Candace Kristina McLean, "'Do This in Memory of Me': The Genealogy and Theological Appropriations of Memory in the Work of Johann Baptist Metz" (PhD diss., University of Notre Dame, 2012), 287.
30. Here my argument about the relation between sainthood and antiblackness resembles that made by George Tinker in the case of the church's missionizing oppression of indigenous peoples: rather than "criticizing [the church's] departed heroes," Tinker writes to "expose the illusion, the covert 'lie' of white self-righteousness as it was internalized and acted on by the missionaries themselves" (George F. Tinker, *Missionary Conquest: The Gospel and Native American Cultural Genocide* [Minneapolis: Fortress Press, 1993], 4–5).
31. *Lumen Gentium*, para. 8. See also Karl Rahner's insistence that "one can no longer in any context of faith maintain that there are sinners 'in' the church as in an external confessional organization but that this carries no implication about the church itself," in Karl Rahner and William F. Gleeson, "The Church of Sinners," *CrossCurrents* 1, no. 3 (1951): 64–74. For more on this, see Leo J. O'Donovan, "A Changing Ecclesiology in a Changing Church: A Symposium on Development in the Ecclesiology of Karl Rahner," *Theologial Studies* 38, no. 4 (1977), 744.
32. Johnson, *Friends of God and Prophets*, 10. See also Alan Neely, "Saints Who Sometimes Were:

church's hagiographical memory from historical scrutiny.[33] If the church does not know who or what it has been, how can it become what it should be?[34]

Utilizing Missionary Hagiography," *Missiology: An International Review* 27, no. 4 (October 1, 1999): 446.

33. Here I critique not what Francis Sullivan describes as "the Tradition with a capital T," that is, the gospel, but the sense of the word tradition that begins with a lowercase t, that is, "the traditionary process." Francis Sullivan, "Catholic Tradition and Traditions," in *The Crisis of Authority in Catholic Modernity*, ed. Michael J. Lacey and Francis Oakley (Oxford: Oxford University Press, 2011), 115. For more on this, see Hippolyte Delehaye, *The Legends of the Saints: An Introduction to Hagiography* (London: Longmans, Green, 1907), 219–20.

34. This critique builds upon the work of other scholars who have called attention to the connection between hagiography and white supremacy: M. Shawn Copeland, *The Subversive Power of Love: The Vision of Henriette Delille* (New York: Paulist Press, 2008); Molly H. Bassett and Vincent W. Lloyd, *Sainthood and Race: Marked Flesh, Holy Flesh* (New York: Routledge, 2014).

1

Sainthood and Historical Memory

To many, it may seem as though this book judges all of these holy men, but especially Claver, too harshly. In particular, some may doubt our capacity to make moral critiques of those who lived before us. They would not be the first to do so. In this way, for example, in her 1896 hagiography, the English nun Maude Dominica Mary Petre sought to acquit Claver on the grounds of historical context when she explained that "even among the most famous philanthropists of the day, there is no positive condemnation of slavery as such."[1] Ultimately, she concludes, "It is always a difficult and doubtful matter to compare the tendencies of different ages."[2] Petre is right. We should not condemn our antecessors simply because they express moral beliefs that have fallen out of fashion. Sensitive to these concerns, this book does not take any of these saints out of his context. In fact, in the case of Claver, accounting for his historical context does not soften our assessment of him; when we attend to his historical context, Claver appears more culpable, not less so. Ultimately, however, this book is

1. Maude Dominica Mary Petre, *Aethiopum Servus: A Study in Christian Altruism* (1896; repr., Memphis, TN: General Books, 2010), 86.
2. Ibid., 175.

uninterested in determining the extent to which Claver is culpable for his own racial conditioning. More than it wishes to blame Claver for his antiblackness supremacy, this book strives to name it as such.

In saying this, I do not claim to take a view from nowhere; I admittedly evaluate all of these men through the lens of my own particularity as a white, U.S.–American, female, cradle Catholic. But have not all Catholics considered the saints from the perspective of their own particularity? It could not be otherwise. Sainthood stories are filtered through the particular subjectivities of the communities that tell them. In this way, sainthood always emerges as a relational endeavor between the person being remembered and the community that remembers her.[3] We do not receive the saints as though they were fragile collectibles preserved forever behind packaging that can never be opened. We inherit them by reinterpreting them; we inherit them *only* if we reinterpret them. This holds especially true in the case of Claver since we know him almost exclusively from the stories others told about him after his death.[4] We do not receive the saints as though they were fragile collectibles preserved forever behind packaging that can never be opened. We inherit them by reinterpreting them; we inherit them *only* if we reinterpret them. Recognizing this, successive generations of Catholics have adapted Claver to their particular sociohistorical contexts. We cannot then exonerate Claver's sainthood simply by pointing out that he inhabited a world that differs from our own. Besides, if we cannot make negative judgments about saints who inhabited foreign cultural contexts, then how can we make positive claims about them? If cultural difference barred us from condemning Claver for his vices, then how could we praise him for his virtues? If historical distance makes a human life untranslatable, then how can Claver's sainthood mean anything to us at all?

We should disregard what I term the historical-context defense for another reason as well. Especially in the post-Tridentine era, individual

---

3. Paola Vargas Arana, "Pedro Claver y la evangelización en Cartagena: Pilar del encuentro entre africanos y el Nuevo Mundo, siglo XVII," *Fronteras de la historia* 11 (2006), 298.
4. Anna María Splendiani, "Un jesuita y una cuidad: Pedro Claver y Cartagena de Indias," t.l, mecanografiado (Bogotá: Colciencias, 2000), 28.

women and men have been elevated to sainthood precisely because they possessed extraordinary virtues. Saints could do what everyone should do better than anyone could. We cannot therefore defend a saint by labeling her a woman of her time. This would be like arguing that a certain basketball player should be elected to her sport's hall of fame because, although she was not that great at many parts of the game, she was no worse at these skills than the average woman of her era. Perhaps even more importantly, this strategy confuses the answer and the question. Rather than simply pointing out that many whites in Claver's day harbored antiblack sentiments, we ought to ask both why what Vincent Lloyd terms "proper racial practice" has not been considered a core saintly virtue, and why the church has so often mistaken racial vice for racial virtue.[5] Put another way, why must Claver be extraordinary in certain ways, but not in the case of his racial comportment?

1.1 Whose Norms? Antiblackness Supremacy and Historical Judgment

We ought to reject calls to exonerate Claver by citing the purported commonness of his racial views for still another reason. This defense unwittingly asserts the normativity of whiteness and erases black people from the historical record. Indeed, few of Claver's white contemporaries have left a written record of opposing black slavery.[6] But many of Claver's black contemporaries left evidence of opposing slavery, despite often lacking access to the written word.[7] In this way, palenques, which were stable settlements of escaped black slaves, dotted the forested countryside surrounding Cartagena even before Claver's arrival there.[8] African-descended residents of Cartagena

---

5. Bassett and Lloyd, *Sainthood and Race*, 4.
6. Arana, "Pedro Claver y la evangelización en Cartagena," 254–55.
7. This does not mean Cartagena's African-born residents were illiterate. Many of them brought their ability to read and write, sometimes in more than one language, over with them from their communities in West and Central Africa. Pablo Fernando Gómez Zuluaga, "Bodies of Encounter: Health, Illness, and Death in the Early Modern African-Spanish Caribbean" (PhD diss., Vanderbilt University, 2010), 79.
8. Marco Palacios and Frank Safford, *Colombia: País fragmentado, sociedad dividida. Su historia* (Bogotá,

denounced slavery every time they ran away from their masters or fought to preserve their independence. Serving as confessor to a group of recaptured *palenqueros* before their execution, Claver knew these places existed.[9] More subtle evidence of black dissent—acts of resistance and creative survival—lay all around him. Indeed, during his ministry in Cartagena, the black population outnumbered the white.[10] Therefore, it may actually have been the case that acceptance of slavery was the minority view. To defend Claver in this way is to say that only the views of white people matter. Why should the moral beliefs of literate Spanish and Creole colonists carry more weight than those of their black contemporaries?

This move also falsely makes the establishment of antiblackness supremacy seem like an inevitability rather than the consequence of countless human choices. Even during Claver's lifetime, Catholic moral theology already possessed the theoretical resources to condemn black slavery as unjust. In fact, while the so-called discovery of the so-called New World did present Spanish and Portuguese Catholics with new theological problems that required theological innovation, this was not the case with African slavery. In order to condemn African slavery, a cleric like Claver, trained in Catholic theology, would need only to apply existing moral frameworks, not devise new ones. For example, although no Christian author had yet issued a categorical condemnation of slavery per se, Catholic moral codes condoned slavery, only under a very specific set of rules, which specified that human beings could be taken as slaves justly only as punishment for conducting an unjust war, committing a capital offense, or falling into debt.[11] Yet many of the women and men who were kidnapped and

Colombia: Grupo Editorial Norma, 2005), 132; Jane Landers, "La Cultura Material De Los Cimarrones: Los Casos De Ecuador, La Española, México Y Colombia" in *Rutas De La Esclavitud En África Y América Latina*, ed. Rina Cáceres (San José, Costa Rica: Editorial de la Universidad de Costa Rica, 2001), 150–52.

9. Arana, *Pedro Claver y la evangelización en Cartagena*, 312.
10. Zuluaga, *Bodies of Encounter*, 2, 22.
11. John T. Noonan, *A Church That Can and Cannot Change: The Development of Catholic Moral Teaching* (Notre Dame, IN: University of Notre Dame Press, 2005), 80–86; David G. Sweet, "Black Robes and 'Black Destiny': Jesuit Views of African Slavery in 17th-Century Latin America," *Revista de Historia de América* 86 (1978): 93.

trafficked to Cartagena fit none of these categories and were snatched up from the ordinary rhythm of their everyday lives, including children who were stolen away while playing. When Claver's white contemporaries used Christian theology to defend the slave trade, they did so only by ignoring certain aspects of long-standing moral theology, such as the rules concerning slavery.

Despite Claver's presumed familiarity with Catholic moral theology, we have no record of Claver's ever wondering about the legitimacy of even a single African person's enslavement. Claver's lack of concern about this matter distinguished him from his mentor Sandoval, who at least "was puzzled over whether or not African slaves were taken captive in a just war" and therefore felt moved to "consult [one of] the leading Jesuit moral theologians of his time," Fr. Luis Brandon, rector of the Jesuit College in Luanda, Angola, about the status of these arriving captives. Father Brandon warned Sandoval that "no Negroe will admit to being a just captive, so [you] ought not ask them whether they are fair captives or not, because they will always say they were stolen or captured under a bad title, understanding that in this way their liberty will be granted."[12] Seemingly, for Claver as for Sandoval, the word of a white man was all that was needed to make a black man a slave. Claver's enthusiastic embrace of slavery reflects less the limitations of the medieval Catholic tradition he inherited than his decision to interpret that tradition through the lens of the relatively recent innovation of antiblackness supremacy.

But even if we were to grade on a historical curve, Claver still would fall below the benchmark set by other white Catholics. Although they almost never did, white people could condemn black slavery, even in Claver's lifetime.[13] Indeed, more than a half century before Claver initiated his ministry, another Spanish-born Catholic priest, Bartolome de las Casas, would recognize, albeit belatedly, the unjust character of

12. Kristen Block, "Faith and Fortune: Religious Identity and the Politics of Profit in the Seventeenth-Century Caribbean" (PhD diss., Rutgers University, 2007), 92.
13. Peter Wade, *Blackness and Race Mixture: The Dynamics of Racial Identity in Colombia* (Baltimore: Johns Hopkins University Press, 1995), 30. Martin A. Klein, *Historical Dictionary of Slavery and Abolition*, 2nd ed. (Lanham, MD: Rowman & Littlefield, 2014), 39.

the slave trade that Claver celebrated. One also wonders how Claver can be considered the "patron saint of racial justice," when other racially flawed and limited white men like Las Casas and Antonio de Valdivieso, the bishop of Nicaragua who was assassinated by white settlers in 1550 because of his defense of Indians, are not even saints.[14]

1.2 Apologizing for Claver: Anachronism and Exoneration

Claver's hagiographers further excuse his acceptance of the slave trade by insisting that he did so only out of a fervent love for the well-being of black souls.[15] In this way, Petre contends that Claver was "so consumed with the desiring of raising and ennobling individual hearts and minds, that he thought little of the social question" surrounding slavery's morality.[16] But Claver's purported dedication to saving souls does not make his embrace of black slavery more acceptable. At least one other prominent Spanish Catholic cleric, Bartolome de Albornoz, recognized that not even the soul-saving gift of baptism could justify African enslavement.[17] Even the Portuguese bishop of the Cape Verde Islands, Frei Pedro Brandão, attempted to end the slave trade; while Claver baptized Africans into slavery, Bishop Brandão "proposed that blacks should be baptized and then set free."[18] Further debunking the myths of moral progress that undergird hagiographical excuse-making, these protests occurred at least twenty and sometimes as many fifty years before Claver began his ministry.[19] But we do not remember any of these men as heroes. Indeed, if it truly was nearly impossible for white people to recognize that Africanized slavery was

---

14. Luis N. Rivera, *A Violent Evangelism: The Political and Religious Conquest of the Americas* (Louisville, KY: Westminster John Knox, 1992), 269. The Nicaraguan bishops did not begin promoting the memory of Valdivieso until the year 2000. Hans-Jürgen Prien, *Christianity In Latin America* (Leiden: Brill, 2012), 124.
15. For a very recent example of this defense, see Ondina E. González and Justo L. González, *Christianity in Latin America: A History* (New York: Cambridge University Press, 2008), 91.
16. Petre, *Aethiopum Servus*, 74–75.
17. David Brion Davis, *The Problem of Slavery in Western Culture* (New York: Oxford University Press, 1988), 190.
18. Hugh Thomas, *The Slave Trade: The Story of the Atlantic Trade, 1440-1870* (New York: Simon & Schuster Paperbacks, 1997), 147.
19. Davis, *Problem of Slavery*, 189; Thomas, *Slave Trade*, 147.

evil as Claver's defenders insist, then should these men not be among the church's most revered saints?

These exemplars notwithstanding, Claver's single-minded concern for the souls of black slaves also seems and well-intentioned, if misguided, largely because we project contemporary understandings of the relation between church and state back onto seventeenth-century imperial Spain. In truth, when Claver sought to Christianize African souls, he was not acting with holy disregard for the things of this world in the way that modern interpreters have tended to assume. While medieval Christians believed "spiritual goals . . . [to be] superior to temporal and civil ones," they did not deem them unrelated. This holds particularly true in the case of missionaries like Claver.[20] For him, there was no pure religion: in defending Catholic orthodoxy, he believed that he was also defending Spanish sovereignty. For the Spanish state, Christianization and conquest were deeply aligned and interdependent projects.[21] Evidencing this understanding, one of Claver's peers explained that "heresy . . . is such that if it is not stopped and uprooted altogether when it is first germinating, it would not merely be harmful to religion, but could totally pervert and subvert the political state." For this reason, he concluded, "In no republic that is Catholic and well governed should diversity of religions be allowed."[22]

This background helps to explain why the Spanish monarchy paid for Claver's initial voyage to Cartagena.[23] In addition to "giving economic aid to the missionaries who penetrated the New World," the Spanish government also paid for Claver's initial voyage from Spain to Cartagena.[24] Claver likely did prioritize the spiritual over the temporal as his hagiographers claim, but his spiritual activities undoubtedly served to consolidate Spanish imperial power. Those who attempt to exonerate Claver by portraying him as single-mindedly devoted to the

---

20. Tinker, *Missionary Conquest*, 17.
21. Rivera, *Violent Evangelism*, 54.
22. Ibid., 54–55.
23. Arana, *Pedro Claver y la evangelización en Cartagena*, 310; Emanuel J. Abston, "Catholicism and African Americans: A Study of Claverism, 1909–1959" (Florida State University, 1998), 81.
24. Emanuel J. Abston, "Catholicism and African Americans: A Study of Claverism, 1909–1959" (Florida State University, 1998), 81.

salvation of souls rather than the establishment of a certain political order, interpret him not charitably, but anachronistically.

We also interpret Claver anachronistically when we interpret his zeal for the liberation of black souls as evidence of his opposition to racial hierarchy either in this world or the next. Just because Claver believed that the slave master's authority did not extend to his slave's soul did not mean he considered black slaves the masters of their own souls. Just as the church's sovereignty over the spiritual realm did not lessen but actually worked in concert with the state's sovereignty over the temporal, Claver's mastery over the souls of black slaves lent support to laymen's ownership of their bodies. Claver worked in cahoots with slave owners and was loved by them. As a friend to slave masters, he was an enemy to the enslaved.

1.3 The Flexible Persistence of Antiblackness Supremacy

But while Claver's context differs from ours in important ways, it also shares much in common with it. Claver's sainthood proves particularly relevant to contemporary Christians precisely because antiblackness supremacy still holds the world together.[25] Shape-shifting according to the historically and geographically specific needs of racialized power, whiteness in contemporary North America undoubtedly differs from whiteness in seventeenth-century Cartagena. But the Spanish-descended residents of Cartagena were no less white than I am just because their whiteness was not identical to mine. Claver would have been habituated into white supremacy even before he stepped foot in America: "By the second half of the fifteenth century, the term 'Negro' was essentially synonymous with 'slave' across the [Iberian] Peninsula."[26]

Claver helped to sustain the social order that accorded whiteness its so-far-uninterrupted inertia: conquest and sovereignty over indigenous people and their land as well as participation in and

25. Wilderson, *Red, White, and Black,* 58.
26. James H. Sweet, "Collective Degradation: Slavery and the Construction of Race," *America* 1492 (2003): 7.

immunity from the slavery imposed solely on people of African descent. Even more, Claver's contemporaries, including those who testified in his beatification proceedings, classified human beings according to a color-coded taxonomy. In addition to calling people of African descent "blacks," they referred to those of European descent as "whites." For example, Claver's best friend and fellow Jesuit Nicholas González names people of African descent as "blacks" more frequently than he identifies them by ethnicity, homeland, language, nativity, religious status, or any of the other terms available to him. When describing the greeting Claver gave the blacks upon their arrival, González recalls how "through the interpreters, he told them that they had come . . . to make sure they were well received in the land of the *whites*."[27] This racial self-identification recurs throughout his testimony. In calling Claver "white," we do not impose upon him an identity that he had not claimed for himself.

Nor have Claver's ecclesial advocates believed him to be racially irrelevant. Since the middle of the nineteenth century, Claver's proponents have promoted him precisely because they perceived an analogy between the racial circumstances of seventeenth-century Cartagena and the United States.[28] Even if these hagiographers defined antiblackness too narrowly, they implicitly conceded the similarities between the racial injustice of Claver's day and that of their own. And they were correct in doing so. All of the Americas suffer from a common antiblackness supremacy, albeit in geographically specific ways.[29] Black slavery and its ongoing afterlife connect our context to Claver's.

27. Anna María Splendiani and Tulio Aristizábal, *El proceso de beatificación y canonización de San Pedro Claver* (Bogotá: Pontificia Universidad Javeriana, 2002), 87. Italics mine. My translation.
28. Nicole von Germeten, "A Century of Promoting Saint Peter Claver and Catholicism to African Americans: Claverian Historiography from 1868–1965," *American Catholic Studies* 116, no. 3 (2005): 23–38.
29. For more on this history, see Walker Grimes, *"Christ Divided:" The Church and the Corporate Vice of Antiblackness* (Minneapolis, MN: Fortress Press, 2017).

2

Claver's Ministry for Slaveocracy

This survey begins with Peter Claver. In addition to his status as the only white saint recognized for ministry to black American slaves, Claver labored in the gory center of the slave trade, the Colombian city of Cartagena, which for centuries served as the sole legal port through which African captives entered the Spanish Americas.[1] The church's memory of Claver also has played a central role in its efforts to evangelize Americans of African descent. In this way, his sainthood both symbolizes the reality of the church's racial past and epitomizes the way it remembers and relates to this past.[2] More than simply offering the most detailed evidence of antiblackness supremacy's vicious presence within the church's corporate body, Claver's sainthood prepares us to perceive the operation of this vice in other hagiographical narratives, such as those of Porres and Toussaint.

For Claver's hagiographers, no aspect of his ministry exemplifies his saintliness more than his purportedly baptizing an estimated three hundred thousand newly arrived African slaves. But Catholics have misinterpreted Claver's baptismal zeal. Misperceiving inclusion in

1. Arana, "Pedro Claver y la evangelización en Cartagena," 302.
2. Bassett and Lloyd, *Sainthood and Race*, 3.

Christian community as inherently opposed to slavery, they have misidentified baptism as slavery's enemy rather than its occasional ally. This is understandable. After all, baptism claims to incorporate individuals in order to grant them both spiritual freedom and eternal life while slavery deprives them of both physical freedom and social life. Claver's commitment to bringing enslaved women and men into the church seems a type of protest of, or at least protection against, the degradation inflicted by slavery. But in truth, a slave master wields power over his slaves to the extent that he manages to hold on to them, both literally and figuratively.[3] Therefore, intimacy alone—even when baptismal—does not defy enslavement; in many instances, it strengthens it. And this proved especially true in the case of Claver's ministry.

2.1 How to Make a Slave: Baptism as Incorporation into Slavery

Claver's baptismal ministry enabled Spanish slave-making processes: it helped to denude African people of their original ties of kinship and community, and then it helped to place them under their masters' power. How? During the days between their watery arrival and their eventual sale, Claver would attempt to strip them of their prior identities and ways of being. Stowed away in warehouses and slave pens, they were a captive audience. Following Ignatius of Loyola's example, Claver believed that "evangelizing new populations consisted in destroying all reason or prior practice." He stated this intention explicitly. Standing in the center of those warehouses and holding pens, he would preach to them, "Just as a serpent sheds his skin, you [Africans] all ought to change your life and customs." For Claver, this entailed that they "strip [themselves] of" what he identified as "gentleness and its vices until you can forget the memory of all of these things."[4] Expressing a supersessionist defense of their enslavement, Claver seemingly used the word "gentleness" as a

---

3. Patterson, *Slavery and Social Death*, 50.
4. Arana, "Pedro Claver y la evangelización en Cartagena," 316. My translation. For two recent arguments that trace the relation between Christian supersessionism and the emergence of white supremacy, see J. Kameron Carter, *Race: A Theological Account* (Oxford: Oxford University Press,

synonym for *heathen*. Yes, baptism ought to confer upon all of its recipients a new identity and requires from them some sort of break with the past. But only Africans and other non-European peoples were compelled to leave not just the stain of original sin but also their social identity behind them. To this end, Claver would assign each black slave he baptized a Spanish name of his choosing.[5] Afterward, he would "make them repeat it . . . putting aside and forgetting the name they had in their own country, because it was the name of a Moor or Gentile and a devil's child."[6]

Although Claver bestowed upon each African captive a new name, he did not provide them names of their own: Claver baptized African survivors of a given slave ship in groups of ten so that he could assign each set the same baptismal name. More than simply stripping them of their individuality, this assembly-line approach to African ministry denied them their family ties. Unlike un-enslaved Christians, African people did not receive their baptismal name from their parents or kinfolk. They had been turned not into children but orphans. Rather than establishing them as Spanish *people*, the acquisition of Spanish names and ways of thinking re-branded them as Spanish *property*. Coercing them to sacramentally "reject . . . [their] own natal community, kinsmen, ancestral spirits, and gods. . . . Claver made it easier for them to be re-possessed and re-purposed by the masters who soon would buy them."[7]

Claver facilitated slave-making processes in a second way. After helping to sever their original ties of kinship, Claver sought to initiate enslave people into a new family, one in which "the Christian God was Father, Jesus was their brother, and Claver was the father figure on earth."[8] In exercising paternal power over the slaves he baptized, Claver did not simply act as a slave master; he made it easier for their eventual owners to act this way as well.[9] Why? To begin with, Claver

2008) and Willie James Jennings, *The Christian Imagination: Theology and the Origins of Race* (New Haven, CT: Yale University Press, 2010).

5. Arana, "Pedro Claver y la evangelización en Cartagena," 52. My translation.

6. Angel Valtierra, *Peter Claver: Saint of the Slaves* (Westminster, MD: Newman, 1960), 114.

7. Ibid., 13, 52, 55.

8. Arana, *Pedro Claver Y La Evangelización En Cartagena*, 311.

could claim paternity over these women and men only because they had been ripped violently from their natural mothers and fathers.[10] Claver's paternal pretensions also were infantilizing. In truth, most enslaved people were not children at the time of their arrival, and all of them already had parents. They lacked parental protection only because they had been kidnapped. Claver's paternity neither supplements nor exists alongside the many and varied bonds of connection they had back in African; it aims to replace them.

Claver would baptize babies who had been born during the Middle Passage without asking for their mothers' permission before doing so.[11] Although hagiographers typically interpret this aspect of his ministry as further proof of his loving service to black slaves, Claver in fact colluded in the kidnapping of black children from their parents. Historical context will not exonerate him. Three centuries earlier, Thomas Aquinas concluded that baptizing the children of unbelievers against their parents' will would be to act "against natural justice if a child, before coming to the use of reason, were to be taken away from its parents' custody, or anything done against its parents' wish."[12] Importantly, Aquinas insists that one cannot remove a child from "the custody of its father, [even] in order to rescue it from the danger of everlasting death."[13] Closer to Claver's time, in 1550 the Episcopal Synod of Lima criticized those Spaniards who would baptize "those [indigenous children] who have not yet the use of reason and are children, without knowing if their parents agree."[14] Perhaps because Claver believed himself "the father of all" the slaves, he considered himself exempt from these decrees.

Claver's fatherhood infantilized enslaved people in another way. Like slaves in all times and places, the women and men Claver baptized could not make their own families, even when these families were spiritual. Their families were instead assigned to them, as Claver would

9. Patterson, *Slavery and Social Death*, 63, 65, 68.
10. Ibid., 311.
11. Splendiani and Aristizábal, *Proceso de beatificación*, 87.
12. Thomas Aquinas, *ST* IIa–IIae, 10, 12, ans.
13. Ibid.
14. Rivera, *Violent Evangelism*, 233.

designate a "Spanish speaking negro or negress of [his or her] own tribe" to serve as godparent to a newly baptized African person.[15] On other occasions, he appointed one of his enslaved translators to this position, ethnic incompatibility notwithstanding.[16] They belonged to whomever Claver said they did. Claver's claims of fatherhood further served slavery by masking its violence. Because he positioned himself as a father, he could misconstrue slavery as a form of adoption. In this way, he assured newly arrived African captives who huddled in fetid holding pens that they "were very fortunate to have been brought to the countries of the Spanish . . . because now [they] could become Christians and his children."[17] Claver's fatherly self-image has appeared saintly only because so many interpreters have misunderstood what makes slavery evil. As Patterson recognizes, enslaved people are not outcasts but captives; they are violently held rather than expelled.[18]

Slavery incorporates its victims into their masters' families not to accord them protection, but to strip them of it. So did Claver's baptismal practices. During Claver's era, Catholics ordinarily used baptism as a way of making spiritual families. But these families were no less socially real than natural families: for example, people related by baptism could not inter-marry.[19] Godparents protected and championed their godchildren; they showered them with baptismal gifts.[20] Godparents also served as *comadres* and *copadres* to birth parents.[21] But many of the African people that Claver baptized shared their godfather with hundreds and perhaps even thousands of enslaved people: Claver's enslaved assistants had numerous godchildren. In addition to lacking the social capital to act as un-

15. Valtierra, *Peter Claver*, 114.
16. Ibid., 107.
17. Splendiani and Aristizábal, *Proceso de beatificación*, 10, 65.
18. Patterson notes that this holds true for all slaves except for the rare case of temple slavery. *Slavery and Social Death*, 48.
19. Ibid., 13.
20. Guido Alfani and Vincent Gourdon, *Spiritual Kinship in Europe, 1500–1900* (Houndmills, Basingstoke, Eng.: Palgrave Macmillan, 2012), 3, 20, 22; Sidney W. Mintz and Eric R. Wolf, "An Analysis of Ritual Co-parenthood (Compadrazgo)," *Southwestern Journal of Anthropology* 6, no. 4 (December 1, 1950): 348.
21. Alfani and Gourdon, *Spiritual Kinship in Europe*, 20.

enslaved godparents would, one person certainly could not act as godparent to so many people in any meaningful sense or "socially thick" sense. Claver's baptismal ministry deprived enslaved people of many of the benefits that ecclesial kinship ordinarily provided.

Claver's baptismal ministry incorporated enslaved people into God's family but did not make them full as only partial members in yet another way. Ordinarily, baptism grants Christians access to the other sacraments. But enslaved people often could receive the other sacraments only if and how their masters allowed. This held especially true in case of matrimony. And although Claver encouraged masters to let their property get married, he did little to ensure that black people enjoyed the rights that this sacrament accorded un-enslaved couples. As "in all slaveholding societies," enslaved black spouses in Cartagena "could be and were forcibly separated."[22] So enslaved women in Cartagena, like enslaved women everywhere, "were obliged to submit sexually to their masters."[23] Even when slaves were allowed to enter into sexual relationships, their sexuality, like their bodies, belonged not to themselves or to their spouses, but to their masters.

Nor did marriage grant black slaves custodial rights over their children.[24] Crucially, Patterson points out, "even if such forcible separations [of children from parents] occurred only infrequently, the fact that they were possible and that from time to time they did take place was enough to strike terror in the hearts of all slaves and to transform significantly the way they behaved and conceived of themselves."[25] "The master," Patterson summarizes, "had the power to remove a slave from the local community in which he or she was brought up."[26] Claver did not consider this power to be inherently unjust. Sometimes Claver did spare enslaved people punishment.[27] But he also encouraged white slave masters to sell their slaves if they could not treat them "kindly."[28] Hagiographers typically acclaim Claver

22. Patterson, *Slavery and Social Death*, 6.
23. Ibid.
24. Ibid., 187.
25. Ibid., 6.
26. Ibid.
27. Markoe, *Slave of the Negroes,* 34–35; Splendiani and Aristizábal, *Proceso de beatificación*, 328.

as "the protector of [the black] race . . . [and] the defender of their rights," but in truth Claver believed they had none.[29] He shared the slave master's view: for Claver, enslaved people ultimately belonged not to their families or communities but to their masters.

Claver could not have acted as a true father to enslaved people even if he had fact championed their rights in the ways his hagiographers contend. Even as slavery separates enslaved mothers and fathers from their own children and keeps them from being true children of the people to whom they belong, it artificially suspends slaves in a state of social childhood. Unlike children who eventually attain adulthood or legal majority and enjoy all the rights and obligations of membership in a family, a slave at best qualifies "either . . . as an illegitimate quasi-kinsman or as a permanent minor who never grew up."[30] Since the slave can never truly have a father, he cannot act as one. And since he cannot inherit from a father, he cannot bequeath property or status to a son. Enslavement excises men from socially protected and legally recognized chains of paternity and filiation. Female slaves are similarly denied the dignity and protection their society accords un-enslaved women in their roles as wife, mother, or adult daughter.[31]

Claiming spiritual paternity over enslaved people, Claver attempted to hold them in a state of perpetual ecclesial childhood. Despite ministering in Cartagena for forty years, Claver never attempted to develop black leadership within the church. He did not encourage black people to become sisters, brothers, or fathers. He permitted them to belong to the church as children only. And Claver claimed African people as children so that he could treat them like slaves.

28. Splendiani and Aristizábal, *Proceso de beatificación*, 195.
29. Markoe, *Slave of the Negroes*, 38–39. Slattery describes Claver similarly. See, for example, *Life of St. Peter Claver, S.J.*, 56, 57, 67, 218, 230.
30. Patterson, *Slavery and Social Death*, 63.
31. Ibid., 34–35.

2.2 Claver's Sinister Soteriology: The Middle Passage as Pathway to (Black) Salvation

The preceding analysis may suggest that Claver simply did not realize the consequences of his baptismal practices. Claver's own words, however, tell us otherwise. Claver baptized Africans into slavery intentionally; he expressed his support for black slavery explicitly, explaining to black survivors of the Middle Passage that "it is better to be a captive [in America] than live as a free man in their own country."[32] According to Claver, although the enslaved person's "body suffers hardship in captivity, [her] soul rests in liberty obtained through the water of holy baptism." Claver believed they had been "brought to Cartagena to be freed from slavery" to the devil.[33] He assured black people that "it is better to be a captive [in America] than live as a free man in their own country."

Claver's passion for saving black souls does not justify his commitment to enslaving black people. Although Claver claimed that "the glorious man is he who is the slave of Christ," what he called the "sweet yoke of Christ" fell differently on black bodies than on white.[34] For Claver, only black people had to be slaves in order to be free. Free white people could be slaves of God without also being slaves to other men. Historical context does not let Claver off the hook for this. Only a few years after Claver's death, the protector of the faith, the man appointed by the Sacred Congregation of Rites to play "devil's advocate" at all beatification proceedings, proclaimed "it notorious that through baptism the slaves [to whom Claver ministered] did not obtain freedom."[35] For centuries, Catholics had recognized baptism as a pathway to not just spiritual life but physical freedom, even though they did not always honor this connection in practice. In severing the connection between social freedom and baptism, Claver did not simply regurgitate long-established beliefs; he chose fidelity to the relatively

---

32. Slattery, *Life of St. Peter Claver*, 56.
33. Valtierra, *Peter Claver*, 112–13.
34. William Morgan Markoe, *The Slave of the Negroes* (Chicago: Loyola University Press, 1920), 35.
35. Splendiani and Aristizábal, *Proceso de beatificación*, 542. My translation.

recent innovation of Africanized slavery over fidelity to longstanding Catholic tradition. Even if we could understand why Claver prioritized eternal life over temporal freedom, only antiblackness supremacy can explain why he did this for blacks only.

Ultimately, when Claver baptized newly arrived blacks, he did not simply tolerate the slave trade or seek to wrest some good from its evil as some hagiographers claim. To the contrary, Claver perceived the transatlantic slave trade as both the manifestation of God's will and the precondition for black salvation. Deploying the Middle Passage as a metaphor for faith, Claver preached

> like those who because of their weak capacity could not understand how they arrived to the land of the whites by travelling on a sea so big that it did not have a . . . pathway on which to walk . . . but only the strokes that whites made on parchment, so it went with those things of our holy faith, that while with your little capacity you could not understand, you ought to believe them and observe how God commanded it.[36]

According to the logic of this metaphor, only white people could make the ocean a passage to salvation; Africans reached the promised land only if they were taken there by whites. Navigated by the unfathomable and therefore godlike power of the whites, the Middle Passage mediated the mystery of salvation to the Africans who traveled it. This background casts Claver's love for the slave trade in a new light: "falling to his knees giving thanks to God for having given them a prosperous voyage for the wellbeing of souls," Claver would set about the priestly task of turning the Africans he called "gentiles," the word he used to designate their status as *heathens,* into Christian slaves.[37] The transatlantic passage that Claver greeted as "good news" likely seemed to these African captives as the worst news of their lives.

2.3 Claver's Sacramental Double Standards

Further helping to incorporate African people into slavery, Claver

---

36. Splendiani and Aristizábal, *Proceso de beatificación,* 93. My translation.
37. Kristen Block, *Ordinary Lives in the Early Caribbean: Religion, Colonial Competition, and the Politics of Profit* (Athens: University of Georgia Press, 2012), 29.

performed the sacrament of baptism according to racialized double-standards. According to his slave Andrés Sacabuche, Claver "did not permit any slave to come to receive baptism without washing their head until it was very clean." But witness testimony suggests that he accused only black people of "ordinarily having very dirty heads."[38] Claver's disgust at the unwashed hair of black candidates for baptism likely issued, at least in large part, from an antiblackness supremacist aesthetics that considered hair texture as a marker of racial difference and aesthetic superiority or inferiority. Witness testimony corroborates this interpretation. According to another of Claver's enslaved interpreters, Ignacio angola, Claver would place the following painting on top of the makeshift altar he used to baptize African slaves. It depicted a white Jesuit priest standing at the foot of the cross, collecting the blood that poured out of the crucified Christ's body into a basin. The white priest was shown using this blood to baptize a black male slave who was kneeling at the priest's feet, who reportedly "became very beautiful due to his being baptized." The other black people in the painting, however, were "very ugly because they had not been baptized."[39] For Claver, Christ's blood does not simply save black people; it makes them beautiful.

Claver's own words affirm this reading.[40] Reflecting Sandoval's influence on him, Claver vowed himself *aethiopum semper servus.* English sources typically translate this appellation as "slave of the slaves forever" or "slave of the blacks forever." But if we place Claver's words in his historical context, we ought to instead translate this phrase as "the slave of the Ethiopians forever." According to the racial taxonomy that his mentor Alonso de Sandoval likely taught him, "the Ethiopian . . . was associated with physical and spiritual monstrosity."[41] As a result, when Claver commanded that black people wash their ordinarily dirty hair before receiving the sacrament of baptism, he

---

38. Splendiani and Aristizábal, *Proceso de beatificación*, 104. My translation.
39. Ibid., 106. My translation. Another one of Claver's slaves provides a nearly identical description of this painting (ibid., 109).
40. Alonso de Sandoval, *Treatise on Slavery: Selections from "De instauranda Aethiopum salute,"* ed. and trans. Nicole von Germeten (Indianapolis: Hackett, 2007), 19.
41. Arana, "Pedro Claver y la evangelización en Cartagena," 309. My translation.

enacted his mentor's belief that "although [the Africans] are black, they can be washed clean by the purity and whiteness of Christ's blood."[42] Like Sandoval, Claver links whiteness with cleanness and purity, and blackness with dirtiness and impurity. Claver also contrasts the clean whiteness of Christ's red blood with the filthy blackness of the African body. More than simply adopting his mentor's racialized aesthetics, he accords them theological meaning.

Claver performed baptism as a journey from not just ugliness to beauty and filthiness to cleanness but also from blackness to whiteness. In so doing, he manufactured racial difference sacramentally, linking blackness with ugliness, filthiness, and sinfulness and whiteness with the triumph over all of them. Black people could never pass over from blackness to whiteness entirely, however.[43] Because their bodies could never be white, they could never be free.

Claver ultimately distorted the meaning of baptismal waters. Just as baptism deploys the specific, historically particular waters of the River Jordan and the Red Sea as potent symbols of liberation, so it draws upon water itself as a symbol of life.[44] Boarding docked slave ships still brimming with human cargo, Claver used water to initiate African slaves into not life but Africanized slavery. Of an encounter with a still-shackled African, Claver recalled the captive's visible thirst for a nearby water jar. Immobilized by iron, the enslaved man could not reach this water on his own. Rather than unbinding him, Claver afforded him a small sip of water and then baptized him, saying: "Tell me, my child, do you not remember the great pleasure your body felt when it received that jug of water[?] . . . Well, listen, just as your body was happy because of that water, there will be much more and even greater happiness in which you have there inside your flesh, when they wash your head with the water I am telling you about . . . to take away your sins."[45] Turning life into a type of death, Claver offered the slave water not to give him life but to render him socially

42. Ibid., 16.
43. Ibid., 85.
44. *Catechism of the Catholic Church*, secs. 1218, 1228.
45. Valtierra, *Peter Claver*, 112.

dead. Baptism ought to pronounce liberation and life kindred spirits, essentially connected.[46] But slavery severs this connection, keeping its victims alive only so that they may toil as slaves. Rather than bringing liberation and life, the water Claver offered ushered this man into slavery and death. Claver stood guard at the tomb.

46. *Catechism of the Catholic Church*, sec. 1221.

3

Claver as Race-Making Ally of
Antiblackness Supremacy

We ought to doubt the standard hagiographical account of Claver's benevolence to black slaves for another reason: why would Cartagena's slave-owning elites celebrate a man who allegedly defended the honor and secured the rights of their chattel? Since they did not truly love enslaved people, why would they care if Claver did? In truth, Claver's first white admirers praised Claver for his paternal devotion to the city's enslaved people largely because they believed it kept them safe. They feared black people much more than they cared about them.

In the decades before Claver arrived at Cartagena, the city had suffered a series of insurrections and raids waged by escaped slaves living in *palenques* located outside the city limits. More than simply depleting the city's economic power, runaway slaves threatened its very survival. The white residents of Cartagena were therefore "desperate . . . [to find] a way of making the Africans . . . docile."[1] Claver's ministry appeared to provide it. Terrified by the looming

---

1. Arana, "Pedro Claver y la evangelización en Cartagena," 23. My translation.

prospect of slave insurrection, the city's "Spanish aristocracy" in particular "felt obliged to collaborate in the work of evangelization," including Claver's.[2] Claver's ministry did not threaten slave masters; it comforted them.

Claver protected both the institution of slavery through his role as confessor and counselor. Immediately after he baptized them, Claver told newly arrived Africans that "their [future] master loves them very much," and they therefore ought to "do what he says"; if they obeyed their new master, then "they [would] have a pleasant captivity [and] be happy and well-clothed."[3] In the confessional, Claver encouraged slaves to confess their temptations and incipient plots to run away from their masters and persuaded the recently escaped to return to the service of their masters. And as official confessor to black slaves convicted by the Holy Office of the Inquisition, he helped to keep black slaves in line by "getting the truth out of them."[4] In short, Claver put white supremacist minds at ease. Disturbingly, Claver's post-abolition era hagiographers do not deny his capacity to make black slaves docile —they simply perceive it as evidence of his saintliness. In this way, for example, Slattery explains that "negroes were daily more docile and more industrious . . . under Claver's guidance" and Markoe details his ability to transform black slaves "from men infuriated by wrongs into docile children of the common Father."[5]

Largely due to the ways Claver exercised supervisory power over Cartagena's black slaves, its white inhabitants perceived him not as a lowly servant of the social order but rather an exalted protector of it. For example, Slattery recounts "a report had spread through the Indies . . . that God had revealed to a very holy person His determination of destroying Cartagena had it not been for the merits and prayers of its apostle," Peter Claver.[6] Affirming this, Don Pedro de Zapata, the man

2. Ibid., 323.
3. Valtierra, Peter Claver, 113.
4. Anna María Splendiani, José Enrique Sánchez Bohórquez, and Emma Cecilia Luque de Salazar, Cincuenta años de Inquisición en el Tribunal de Cartagena de Indias, 1610-1660: Documentos inéditos procedentes del Archivo Histórico Nacional de Madrid (AHNM), libro 1020, años 1610-1637 (Bogotá: Centro editorial Javeriano, Instituto colombiano de cultura hispánica, 1997), 2:284.
5. Slattery, Life of Peter Claver, 81, 191; Markoe, Slave of the Negroes, 35, 56.
6. Slattery, The Life of Peter Claver, 211.

who twice served as the governor of the province of Cartagena, shared that "so great and so universally diffused was the reputation of Fr. Claver's sanctity, that he was considered the column and support of the state."[7] Attending more closely to Claver's context again unveils this aspect his sainthood as not benign but aligned with antiblackness supremacy. In the seventeenth century, residents of Cartagena feared not just the Protestant enemies of Catholic Spain but, perhaps even more immediately, the *palenqueros* with whom they remained in a state of vacillating but uninterrupted warfare. More than simply preserving antiblackness supremacy within the city, when Claver reconciled slaves with their masters, dissuaded slaves from running away, or appeared to preempt slave insurrection, Claver also deprived these *palenques* of new members. He protected the city by keeping black people inside of it.

Claver's reputation as a protector of the city spread to those who visited it. In this way, "generals of the army, officers of the navy, and all the most distinguished personages, visited him on the arrival" to this port city.[8] So, too, "the governor of the town together with the nobility often came to recommend to his prayers the preservation of Cartagena and its inhabitants." Like their secular counterparts, "prelates and priests made it their duty to consult him in the most difficult cases of conscience and received his decisions as oracles." And so did slave traders. Verifying his role as a type of patron saint of not just Cartagena, but also the slave trade that sustained it, merchants, many of them involved directly with the trafficking of black flesh, "would not embark without receiving a blessing, and on their return, their first inquiry was after him."[9]

Perhaps largely because of Claver's pacifying capacities, the city's white social elite, including the city's governors and "royal officials," vied for the honor of being the first one to "give him notice" of the arrival of a new "boat of blacks." In exchange, Claver "would celebrate masses for this person as a tip" for his or her service. Other times, he

7. Ibid., 212.
8. Splendiani and Aristizábal, *Proceso de beatificación*, 210. My translation.
9. Ibid., 211. My translation.

gave the person sackcloths and disciplines.[10] As González details, these "important persons" believed that by "participating ... in the penances and mortifications that Father Claver practiced for the spiritual profit of the blacks," they could "win indulgences."[11] Claver qualified as "the saint of the slave trade" for protecting not its victims but the trade itself.[12]

3.1 Claver as Racial Border Patrol

Precisely because it requires "an almost perverse intimacy between master and slave," slavery creates a problem it can never completely solve.[13] A slave master must hold his property close, but the threat of slave insurrection, for example, also impels him to keep them at a certain distance. Slavery also inflicts stigma and dishonor on its victims; slave masters therefore perceive the people they possess as inherently contaminating, especially symbolically. White residents of Cartagena could not exercise masterly power over African people unless they brought them into their homes and city. But Africanized slavery could not survive if the boundary between whiteness and blackness did not. Just as Claver patrolled the consciences of black slaves, so he policed this symbolic racial boundary. In so doing, Claver enabled his white contemporaries to extract power from both blackness and black people without being contaminated by them. For these reasons did his elite contemporaries lauded him as a hero.

The purported repulsiveness of the black body recurs as a central theme in witness testimony. Claver's enslaved interpreter Ignacio de Angola recalls the "innumerable times the blacks defecated on" his cloak because they were suffering from diarrhea.[14] This occurrence would fill Claver not with disgust but delight.[15] His white fellow Jesuit and friend González similarly praises Claver for his defending the right

10. Ibid., 86.
11. Ibid. My translation.
12. Anna María Splendiani, "Un jesuita y una ciudad: Pedro Claver y Cartagena de Indias," t. 1, mecanografiado (Bogotá: Colciencias, 2000), 28.
13. Patterson, Slavery and Social Death, 50.
14. Splendiani and Aristizábal, Proceso de beatificación, 218. My translation.
15. Ibid.

of enslaved black women and men to enter church despite the fact that "they filled it with an intolerable stench."[16] Claver's proximity to black people appeared heroic largely because because their bodies seemed so grotesque.

The words of his mentor provide us reason to believe that Claver himself shared this view. Sandoval believed that "working with slaves will make a person humble" primarily because he considered them to be stupid and ugly. According to Sandoval, black "people are so barbaric that it requires so much work to catechize them and prepare them for baptism and confession, especially when they are cramped by sickness and so disgusting that nature itself abhors them."[17] For Sandoval, black people were not repulsive only when they were ill.[18] According to contemporary historian, Nicole von Germeten, Sandoval "judged the Spanish to be more physically attractive and appealing" than Africans.[19] Ignoring or perhaps oblivious to the routine Spanish rape and sexual abuse of their black slaves, Sandoval assured his audience that "if there is temptation in seeing the blacks naked, that very nakedness and the disgust that goes along with it are a very effective remedy against temptation."[20] The African ministry would also make a white person "kinder, gentler, less selfish, and more patient," ultimately increasing his "chance of going to heaven."[21] So he similarly exhorted the Jesuit order to assume this ministry collectively in order to "receive moral benefits and God's favor."

More than simply noting his capacity to tolerate the purportedly disgusting black body in a way the average man could not, Claver's defenders emphasized the contrast between his body and those of the black slaves to whom he ministered. Not only did Claver never get sick, he also seemingly never got dirty. The enslaved interpreter Ignacio recalls that, despite being defecated on, "somehow his cloak never smelled bad."[22] His nearly miraculous immunity to the physically

16. Ibid., 21. My translation.
17. Ibid., 101.
18. Arana, "Pedro Claver y la evangelización en Cartagena," 307.
19. Germeten, in Sandoval, *Treatise on Slavery*, 97.
20. Ibid.
21. Ibid., 98.

and symbolically contaminating black body persisted even into death: unlike the living body of the slave, which was marked by death, even Claver's "corpse did not smell."[23]

Claver further defended the border between whiteness and blackness due to the way his "mission to the lepers dovetails with his more general reputation as *the slave of the slaves.*"[24] In the seventeenth century Spanish Americas, "colonial perceptions of lepers . . . resemble[d] [the way people envisioned] . . . Africans in the Americas."[25] This association persisted and perhaps even intensified the perceived relationship between blackness and contagion: the *protomedicato* of Cartagena—the early modern version of a public health worker—would inspect slaves for characteristically African diseases such as yellow fever before enslaved people were allowed to be removed from the slave ship.[26] Medical authorities also associated leprosy with not just Africa, but also blackness: one doctor "believed that [leprosy] came entirely from Africa" and that, like racial identity, "it could only be passed mother to child, either in the womb or during lactation."[27] And according to Claver's contemporary, the white barber Don Antonio Montero de Miranda, "blacks . . . were the majority of the . . . patients" at the leper hospital called San Lorenzo.[28]

Partially due to their stigmatizing association with each other, lepers and black people also occupied the same spatial relation to the city: the leper hospital San Lorenzo, like both the black barrio of Getsemani and the city's slave barracks, existed "well beyond the . . . security of the walled portion of the city."[29] Indeed, many of the witnesses who testified about Claver's ministry at San Lazaro made explicit reference to its location "outside the walls of the city." In fact, they spoke this not like a description so much as a title.[30] Like

22. Splendiani and Aristizábal, *Proceso de beatificación*, 218.
23. Ibid., 484. My translation.
24. Germeten, "Problems and Challenges," 17.
25. Ibid., 20.
26. James Ferguson King, "Descriptive Data on Negro Slaves in Spanish Importation Records and Bills of Sale," *The Journal of Negro History* 28, no. 2 (Apr 1943): 208–10.
27. Germeten, "Problems and Challenges," 19.
28. Splendiani and Aristizábal, *Proceso de beatificación*, 261. My translation.
29. Block, *Ordinary Lives in the Early Caribbean,* 29.

an invading contagion, both groups came from outside and were therefore made to remain outside. More than simply believing black people more susceptible to leprosy, seventeenth-century aesthetic habits perceived blackness itself as a form of it.

Claver's ministerial practices linked blackness with leprosy in other ways. Just as Claver would travel out to the docks to tend to newly arrived African slaves, so would he venture out beyond the city walls to comfort the patients of San Lorenzo. Both places were simultaneously symbolically liminal and spatially remote: a docked slave ship held those who would soon be brought inside of the city, but only after the threat they posed had been neutralized; the leper hospital housed those who once resided inside of the city, but were too dangerous to do so any longer. Uniquely able to travel between both worlds, Claver put his priestly powers to good use.

Witnesses recognized the similarities between his ministry to both groups, stressing that, in addition to hugging and caressing both lepers and black people, Claver also comforted and consoled them; he cleaned the faces of both lepers and black people with his cloak, and he made sure to hear their confessions. They described him as covering the indecent bodies of both lepers and black people with various articles of clothing and gifting them food and tobacco. For those who testified at his beatification hearing, leprosy and blackness were not simply two similar maladies; they often co-occurred. According to witnesses, almost all of the lepers Claver visited were black.[31]

Claver's ministry to lepers qualifies as heroic partially due to leprosy's association with blackness. Nicholas González testified that just as Claver "would enter [the leper hospital] as though it were a lush and fragrant garden," despite the fact that "the smell of those contagious with this disease was intense," so "he did the same in the warehouses where the newly arrived blacks were stored," despite that the fact that "there was also great odor, not just because of how many of them were sick with contagious diseases, but also because of the

30. Splendiani and Aristizábal, *Proceso de beatificación*, 252–54, 256, 258, 261, 264–67, 269, 270, 272, 274, 315.
31. Germeten, "Problems and Challenges," 18.

nature of the blacks."[32] Another awe-struck witness recalled Claver's "licking with his tongue some very large [leprous] wounds of a black slave woman in San Lazaro."[33] Just as this woman's blackness becomes more horrific because she has leprosy, so her leprosy becomes more horrific because she is black. Just as Claver receives credit for his ability to stand the stench emitted by black slaves without vomiting or passing out, so he appears superhuman for displaying the same composure in the presence of lepers.

Without recognizing these imaginative connections between blackness and leprosy, we cannot fully understand why Claver's ministry appeared heroic and therefore saintly to his contemporaries. Claver and his contemporaries did not simply believe that black people and lepers were similarly repulsive and contaminating; they imagined blackness as repulsive and contaminating due to its perceived similarities to leprosy. In settling on a story about Claver's holiness, his contemporaries helped to tell a certain story about blackness. In addition to conforming to pre-established racial notions, Claver's hagiography helped to establish them.

But more than simply strengthening imaginative links between black people and lepers, Claver's ministry served to preserve the ideologically important distinctions between them. After all, in seventeenth century Cartagena, leprosy did not render a person inherently enslavable. While Claver and his contemporaries undoubtedly believed that both lepers and blacks could endanger the city by contaminating its inhabitants, only black people were perceived as violent. This helps to account for the small but significant differences between Claver's ministry to both groups. Witnesses never recalled Claver beating, whipping, or berating any of the lepers he visited, despite their needing to confess their sins to him. Second, when witnesses marveled at his willingness to touch and hug lepers, they accentuated his heroism by describing the way in which he would sometimes visit the hospital without wearing his cloak.[34] In stories

32. Splendiani, *Proceso*, 232. My translation.
33. Germeten, "Problems and Challenges," 18.
34. In stark contrast to descriptions of his baptismal interactions with black people, especially men,

detailing Claver's physical proximity to healthy black people, however, witnesses typically make sure to mention the presence of Claver's cloak as evidence of his unfailing modesty. Witnesses describe Claver as physically close to enslaved people, but never uncovered before them. While we can only speculate at the significance of this detail, here witness testimony perhaps betrays a bit of racialized sexual anxiety or self-consciousness about Claver's relation to enslaved people. Sandoval may have considered enslaved black people to be sexually repulsive; Claver's admirers were not so sure.

3.2 Erotic Slaveocracy: Sex and the Lash

Inattention to Claver's historical context can lead us to misunderstand this testimony. González, along with Claver's other early champions, emphasizes his chastity not just because Claver had vowed to uphold it but also because, in his role as priest and confessor, he occupied a position of particular sexual power and notoriety. Due to the sexually charged character of confessing, "priests were directed to hear confessions in an open or public place in the sight of all."[35] Historian Karen V. Powers explains that

> because it was part of Church procedure to inquire into the sexual practices of parishioners during confession, priests had a prime opportunity to guide discussions in the direction of their prurient interests. This often became a way of exciting themselves and ended in inappropriate behaviors and in sexual solicitation in the confessional as well as outside it.[36]

For these reasons, "almost all authorities warn[ed] that when a woman comes to confess, the priest should place her at his side so that he cannot look into her face."[37] Because Claver's renown derived in no small part from his role as confessor, advocates for his beatification,

accounts of his visits to minister to the lepers do not reassure the audience of Claver's modesty and chastity.

35. Thomas N. Tentler, *Sin and Confession on the Eve of the Reformation* (Princeton, NJ: Princeton University Press, 1977), 82.

36. Karen Vieira Powers, *Women in the Crucible of Conquest: The Gendered Genesis of Spanish American Society, 1500-1600* (Albuquerque: University of New Mexico Press, 2005), 200.

37. Tentler, *Sin and Confession*, 82.

especially a Jesuit insider such as González, would have recognized the importance of assuring Vatican officials of Claver's sexual propriety. Any confessor could be perceived as sexually suspicious.

But González most likely realized that it was especially important to establish the modesty of Claver in particular, given the way in which Spanish conquest had heightened the sexual power of priestly confessors. In the seventeenth-century Spanish Americas, "sexual abuse was widespread among the Catholic clergy, especially in the confessional."[38] Further enabling such misconduct, although "many priests were accused of solicitation" during this period, they did not receive punishments severe enough to deter future abuse.[39] So racialized power provides racialized impunity: in seventeenth-century Spanish America, "rape occurred on an unprecedented scale," and "Indian women and African slaves experienced rape to an unparalleled degree." Racialized power dynamics undoubtedly emboldened priestly abusers: if confessors sexually abused not just nuns but even the white wives of Spanish noblemen, how much more frequently must they have levied sexual violence on the most powerless members of society?[40] Spanish whites dominated indigenous and African-descended peoples differently: by its nature, slavery renders enslaved people particularly susceptible to sexual abuse, even compared to other oppressed peoples. Therefore, as confessor to enslaved people, Claver performed the most sexually suspicious clerical task in the presence of the most sexually vulnerable population. If confessors sexually abused not just nuns but even the white wives of Spanish noblemen with impunity, imagine how much more frequently they levied sexual violence on the most powerless members of society. Those seeking to make a case for Claver's sainthood would have been particularly anxious to "avoid all occasion or suspicion of evil."[41]

But González—the witness most concerned with asserting Claver's

38. Karen Vieira Powers, *Women in the Crucible of Conquest: The Gendered Genesis of Spanish American Society, 1500–1600* (Albuquerque: University of New Mexico Press, 2005), 200.
39. Ibid.
40. Ibid., 199.
41. Tentler, *Sin and Confession*, 82.

modesty—unwittingly calls attention to an aspect of Claver's ministry that he likely intends to cover up. González seeks to establish Claver as modest before not just black women but black men as well. According to González, Claver "made the black interpreters cover [the women] ... with ... small robes."[42] Of his sacramental encounters with black men, González explains that "the demureness and modesty of Father Claver was such that," before he would let naked African men kneel before him to receive baptism, he would drape his cloak over their naked bodies and would "stay in his cassock the whole time it was necessary to interrogate them."[43] Because he felt compelled to assure his interviewer that Claver remained in his cassock the entire time he baptized enslaved people of both sexes, González both conceded and drew attention to the sexually suggestive nature of this arrangement. González's testimony also dramatizes the inherently sexually degrading character of the slave trade: enslaved people presumably had been stripped down before being crammed inside the dank belly of a slave ship.

Although González recognized the importance of clearing his friend of sexual misconduct with women, he may have believed it even more important to clear him of sexual misconduct with men. In the Spanish Americas, as elsewhere, enslaved men also suffered sexual violation at staggeringly high rates. Unlike the rape of black female slaves, however, the rape and sexual violation of black male slaves "leaves behind no biological record in the form of offspring." Further erasing their suffering from our memory, prevailing ideologies of masculine impenetrability have rendered these male slaves "even more constrained than female slaves from verbalizing the experience of sexual abuse."[44] But, just as in cases of heterosexual rape, homosexual rape typically was committed by the more powerful against the less powerful. A survey of the Inquisition records of New Spain reveals that "wealthier men in positions of authority were more likely to seek

42. Ibid.
43. Splendiani and Aristizábal, *Proceso de beatificación*, 350. My translation.
44. Robert Richmond Ellis, "Reading through the Veil of Juan Francisco Manzano: From Homoerotic Violence to the Dream of a Homoracial Bond," *PMLA* 113, no. 3 (May 1, 1998): 422–35.

sexual favors from younger, less powerful males."[45] If colonial-era priests used the confessional to sexually coerce enslaved black women, so too must at least some of these priests have inflicted sexual abuse on enslaved black men.

Further affirming the reality of clerical sex with subordinate males both free and enslaved, the historiographical record of colonial Latin America abounds with "examples . . . of slaves who had sex with slaveholders in workshops and haciendas and priests who had sex with novices and male confessants."[46] But "even when the [homosexual] acts were purported to have taken place with a priest . . . the Inquisition typically did not put the priest on trial or take any direction action against" him "unless the priest was a repeat offender."[47] Inquisition records suggest that priests also abused enslaved boys. For example, "the mother of a thirteen-year-old mulatto servant boy . . . denounced" a priest for "hugging her son, kissing him, and taking off his pants while trying to convince him that while it was a sin for a man and a woman to engage in the 'carnal act,' it was not so for two men."[48]

This historical context pertains to Claver's sainthood because his role as confessor accorded him intimacy with black men: witness testimony suggests that Claver confessed the sins of white women in their homes and the sins of black people at the Jesuit College.[49] While Claver confessed the sins of black women during the day, he administered this sacrament to black men at night in a private room inside the Jesuit College. During Lent, black men also frequently slept overnight at the College so that Claver could hear their confessions in the wee hours of the morning.[50]

But Claver did not merely hear the confessions of black slaves; he also owned some. Claver lived in close proximity to both his enslaved translators and the other people his Jesuit order owned; this proximity

---

45. Lee Michael Penyak, "Criminal Sexuality in Central Mexico, 1750–1850" (PhD diss., University of Connecticut, 1993), 275.
46. Zeb Joseph Tortorici, "Contra Natura: Sin, Crime, and 'Unnatural' Sexuality in Colonial Mexico, 1530–1821" (PhD diss., University of California, 2010), 136.
47. Ibid., 222.
48. Ibid., 233.
49. Splendiani and Aristizábal, *Proceso de beatificación,* 350, 178–79.
50. Ibid., 180.

rendered these slaves especially susceptible to sexual abuse.[51] Claver's enslaved translators in particular were even more sexually vulnerable since they came under his power while they were young boys, immediately upon their arrival to Cartagena. If the "mulatto servant boy" memorialized in the Inquisition records allegedly suffered abuse even though he had a mother to defend him, imagine how sexually vulnerable Claver's hand-picked child translators were: they had been deprived of all family ties.[52] We do not need to accuse Claver of sexual abuse of his or anyone else's male slaves in order to place claims about his sexual virtue in their historical context. Especially in his role as slave master, Claver occupied a position that was inherently rather than accidentally sexually exploitive.

51. Arana, "Pedro Claver y la evangelización en Cartagena," 312.
52. Splendiani and Aristizábal, *Proceso de beatificación*, 180. For more on what she calls "the strong homoerotic component . . . [of] Catholic sacramentality," see Tina Beattie, *New Catholic Feminism: Theology and Theory* (New York: Routledge, 2006), 116–20.

4

The Racialized Humility of Peter Claver

In addition to his prolific sacramental accomplishments, Claver's hagiographers submit his superhuman humility as the strongest evidence for his saintliness. In particular, these advocates proclaim Claver the "slave of the slaves" because he engaged in acts of service and self-debasement.[1] Claver perceived himself similarly, aspiring to be "the slave of the negroes forever."[2] But, in declaring Claver the slave of the slaves, we speak the impossible. A master-less slave is no slave at all. Claver was not a slave to black people because they were not empowered to act as his masters. The sociopolitical conditions of seventeenth-century Colombia rendered this racial role reversal inconceivable. Nor did Claver sincerely desire to trade places with black slaves. Unlike enslaved people, Claver chose his slavery and could exit from it at his own discretion: as a Spanish-born white man, he enjoyed a freedom he deemed unnecessary for the blacks he claimed to serve.

Claver's admirers often posit his commitment to self-mortification as evidence of his humility and self-sacrifice. Contemporary supporters

1. Valtierra, *Peter Claver*, 280–83.
2. *The Catholic Encyclopedia*, s.v. "St. Peter Claver," New Advent, http://tinyurl.com/hepegmr.

may also perceive it as a show of solidarity with the enslaved. Yet even this purportedly servile self-discipline only served to reinforce the racialized line between slave and master. Attending more carefully to Claver's context enables us to understand why. In seventeenth-century New Granada, Hispanic Catholics associated self-mortification with holiness. Affirming the existence of a thoroughly interconnected cosmos, they believed the human body served as a site of "mediation between the self and the soul, between the material and the spiritual," as well as between the individual and the social.[3] For them, punishment of the body enabled one not simply to imitate Christ but to experience true union with him.[4] In a similar way, they believed that one accessed the soul through the body: when one punishes the body, she purifies the soul; inversely, "in bringing the body to its limits" through severe self-punishment, one "demonstrates the strength of one's soul."[5] In transforming the body into a vessel of pain rather than pleasure, many seventeenth-century Hispanic residents of New Granada believed they could "open a path for the spiritualization of the body."[6] In cleansing oneself of individual sin in this way, one also decontaminated the social order. More than simply self-denying, self-mortification was perceived as socially therapeutic and protective.[7]

Although Claver's nightly, self-mortifying practices were intense and painful, they differed substantially from the disciplining violence enslaved people would have endured. First, because Claver was used only if he allowed himself to be used, he was not really used in the way a slave is. Second, Claver chose to bind himself in vows of obedience while a slave is captured against her will. Third, more than simply resulting from his own will and free decision, Claver's self-mortifying practices operated as a scheme of self-mastery. Unlike a slave who is whipped by another person against her will and in order to make her submit to the will of her master, Claver hit himself on his own

---

3. Jaime Humberto Borja, "Cuerpo y mortificación en la hagiografía colonial neogranadina," *Theologica Xaveriana* 57, no. 162 (2007): 262–65, http://tinyurl.com/hvma3kx.
4. Ibid., 268.
5. Ibid., 273.
6. Ibid., 278.
7. Ibid., 273.

accord and in order to make himself the master of his own body. Claver's self-mortification differs from the abuses endured by the city's enslaved population in a fourth way: While the slave's susceptibility to corporal punishment renders her dishonorable, Claver's penitential actions accorded him great honor. In fact, those like Claver who achieved the highest level of mortification were considered "perfect."[8] In a similar way, Claver's penitential achievements revealed him to his contemporaries as a man of great power; in contrast, an actual slave qualifies as uniquely disempowered precisely because he suffers corporal punishment at the hands of a master outside of himself.

Fifth, unlike the millions of Africans who died in stinking slave ships on transatlantic passages, in the sweltering cane fields of the Caribbean, or under the searing sharpness of a slave master's whip, Claver received a lavish funeral mass filled to the brim with admirers. Slattery describes the treatment his corpse received: "From all the churches in the town were sent beautiful tapestries and hangings to decorate the altar and tomb," civic leaders fought for the honor of carrying the "precious burden" of his body, and assembled crowds "rushed . . . to kiss his hands and feet."[9] Further unlike the abused bodies of living black slaves or the corpses of transported Africans that lay discarded on the floor of the Atlantic, Claver's corpse was adored and cared for.[10] Claver's sainthood reveals an unsettling ecclesial double standard: when a white man playacts the degraded status of a slave, we honor him as a saint, but when black women and men languish as true slaves, we disregard them.

Claver's regimen of self-mortification ought to trouble us not because such practices have fallen out of fashion; rather, like other aspects of his ministry, it appears more disturbing once we place it within its historical context. Claver's practices of piety enacted antiblackness supremacy precisely because they obeyed the theological and cultural logic of his historical context. In recovering and reconstructing this context, we better position ourselves to

8. Ibid., 270.
9. Slattery, *Life of St. Peter Claver*, 232.
10. Ibid., 232–34.

appreciate the antiblack character of Claver's ministry as well as his saintly afterlife.

4.1 A Slave Master, Not a Slave

More than merely failing to live up to the title of "slave of the slaves forever," Claver in fact acted like a type of slave master. Rather than descending into degrading humility as his hagiographers claim, Claver actively sought and thoroughly enjoyed the privileges and honor of white mastery. And while he denied himself many pleasures, especially those related to food and physical comfort, he did not shun the pleasures of antiblackness supremacy. Nor did Claver serve Cartagena's slaves as much he demanded that they submit to his will. I make these claims for the following reasons: first, Claver owned his interpreters; they were purchased by the Jesuit *colegio* at his command and for the purpose of serving his needs. Nor did Claver did receive these slaves passively. Experiencing the pleasure of surveying black flesh, he chose his slaves himself. Paola Vargas Arana recreates the process by which Claver purchased them:

> The juveniles, all boys, were selected by the Jesuit, before the ships would anchor in the port. Together with a group of interpreters, he would enter in the slave hold and ask them to ask which of the slaves could speak more than two languages. This is how he determined who would serve him.[11]

Further discrediting claims of Claver's exceptional humility, Claver did not simply buy black flesh; he enjoyed first dibs on the bidding for it. After Claver had made his selection, "he would request that the *colegio* purchase that slave with the unique purpose of serving his evangelizing project."[12] Other times, Claver would rent out slaves' labor, "paying to their owners the salary for the days that they were employed in this ministry."[13] Epitomizing slave mastership, Claver made slaves an instrument of his will, making them whatever he needed them to be.

11. Arana, "Pedro Claver y la evangelización en Cartagena," 311. My translation.
12. Ibid., 312. My translation.
13. Splendiani and Aristizábal, *Proceso de beatificación*, 86. My translation.

Second, Claver in fact participated at both ends of the slave trade. Perhaps unsatisfied with the linguistic abilities of the slaves who happened to arrive in his city, Claver "gave to one of his friends, who was going to Guinea, sufficient money to purchase three of the most docile and intelligent Negroes he could find."[14] In addition to purchasing slaves already stolen, Claver acted as their trafficker. Belying claims of Claver's humility, Claver possessed power over black flesh that the majority of white men lacked.

Third, when Claver did not participate directly in the buying and selling of black flesh, he served as the trade's great cheerleader. Claver loved the transatlantic slave trade so fiercely that "whenever a privateer sailed for Guinea, he begged to be conveyed to its barbarous coasts, that he might penetrate the vast countries of Africa, and subject them to the law of Jesus Christ." Unable to help kidnap and transport Africans himself, "he entreated the captains to bring him all the Negroes they could, that he might instruct them."[15] Claver acted as Christ's slave catcher. In slave catching for Christ, he believed African women and men could be free only if they remained slaves. More than simply cheering for the slave trade, Claver also seemed to act like its patron saint, providing it miraculous protection. On his way to Guinea to purchase slaves for Claver, his slave-trading friend ran into a violent storm, which caused his ship to sink. Trusting in Claver's power to supernaturally protect him, "he wrapped the money that Claver had entrusted to him for the purchase around his body [and] plunged into the sea." As if evidencing Claver's protective power, the slave merchant washed up on shore physically unharmed and bereft of all his possessions except for Claver's money. Miraculously in his view, he managed to keep his promise to Claver, buying three slaves on his behalf.[16] More than simply buying slaves for Claver, this merchant could buy them because of him.

Claver acts as a slave master in a fourth way: although Claver's slaves performed much of the spiritual labor, Claver alone receives the credit

14. Ibid., 138.
15. Slattery, *Life of St. Peter Claver*, 183.
16. Splendiani and Aristizabal, *Proceso de beatificación*, 138. My translation.

for it. Like a ventriloquist, Claver's ownership of their bodies allowed him to speak languages he did not know. These slave interpreters, ostensibly owned by the College but dedicated entirely to Claver's use, helped in "the collection of alms" for the presumably unenslaved poor; they also played music at mass and made the medallions "that Claver would give to the other Africans."[17] In addition to assisting in the catechizing of black slaves, they also served as extra godparents to them.

Further positioning Claver as a slave master, several of Claver's slave interpreters imply that more than simply working alongside Claver, they often worked in his place. For example, Claver's slave Ignacio Sosa recalls that when his slaves alerted him to the arrival of a slave ship, "if he could not go personally to help the slaves disembark, he sent the interpreters to do it" on their own.[18] How frequently did this occur? Another one of Claver's slaves, Francisco Yolofo, reports that "the first two or three years that he knew Father Peter Claver, [Claver] would accompany [his interpreters] to give a welcome to the blacks." But eventually "the rectors of the College ordered [Claver] not to be at the ships because he was old and tired." From that moment on, only Claver's slaves visited newly arrived slave ships.[19] Since Yolofo worked as Claver's slave for twenty two years, from the time he first arrived in Cartagena in chains in 1634 until Claver's death in 1654, we can conclude that, for at least nineteen years of Claver's ministry, Claver did not perform the tasks for which he is most renowned.

This erasure of his co-ministers' personhood epitomizes the master-slave relation. As "human surrogates," Claver's interpreters existed as an "extension of [his] power." For this reason, Patterson explains, "the real sweetness of mastery for the slaveholder lay not immediately in profit, but in . . . the realization that at one's feet is another human creature who lives and breathes only for one's self," who exists "as a surrogate for one's power [and] . . . a living embodiment of one's manhood and honor." Because one need not extract economic profit

17. Ibid., 312. My translation.
18. Ibid., 258. My translation.
19. Ibid., 114. My translation.

42

from a slave in order to profit from one's mastership over her, Claver's voluntary poverty did not prevent him from acting as a master of black slaves.[20]

This held especially true in the case of Africanized slavery. The Africanization of slavery forged an association between blackness and slave status. As a result, even lower status white people were positioned as masters of all black people, sharing in the pleasures, power, and honor of mastership even if they owned no slaves. Helping to preserve this association, Claver enacted mastership over not just his personal slaves but also all of Cartagena's black women and men. Claver situated the city's black slaves in a state of manufactured and dishonorable dependence, thereby amplifying his own power and honor. Claver appeared heroic only because black people were considered to be both disgusting and dangerous. Believing himself the master of all black flesh, Claver began to violently discipline enslaved Africans almost immediately after their arrival to Cartagena. Claver would continue to inflict violence on black people long after they left the city's docks and slave pens, beating adult women and men with a large crucifix, flaying them with a whip, and stealing their possessions, when they danced, grieved, or interacted in ways he decried as sinful. To him, the undisciplined black body appeared demonic and dangerous, especially in public.

But Claver's concern for public order proved highly racialized. While he whipped the disobedient bodies of black women and men without warning, he treated publicly raucous whites quite differently. If, while cruising the city's plazas and public places, he encountered "a table where cards were being played, he would come up to them and when the players were Spanish people and white, he would say to them with great peace and love, 'My Lords, entertain yourself and enjoy yourself a little bit, but don't swear.'"[21] Claver did encourage the city's white residents he encountered in public places to comport themselves in a Christian manner, but perhaps because he believed whites were

20. Patterson, *Slavery and Social Death*, 78.
21. Ibid., 191.

fundamentally reasonable in a way his black subjects were not, he never subjected white people to the lash.[22] Regardless of Claver's conscious beliefs, his racially differentiated disciplining practices affirmed and upheld the antiblackness supremacist social order.

And while he sought to prevent black people from gathering in public spaces on their own terms, either to mourn or to dance, he encouraged them to occupy public spaces under his direction. According to Sacabuche, on Lenten Sundays,

> Claver would process through the streets of the city under a double-colored taffeta banner and with a cross in his hand . . . reciting Christian doctrine while calling on all of the blacks that he encountered along the way to accompany him in the procession.[23]

Then, he would bring these slaves to the Plaza of the Yerba, the very site where they engaged in the dances and grieving ceremonies that Claver would violently interrupt, in order to publicly test their knowledge about Christian doctrine.[24] As if seeking to re-create the physical space of the plaza by replacing African forms of embodiment with Spanish ones, Claver "would get up on a table and fervently preach to the assembled slaves about the use of their souls and that they ought to seek to be good and to serve both God and their masters to the best of their ability."[25] Bringing the spatial *re-conquista* to completion, Claver would then lead them "back to the Church where he made them say an act of contrition" and "heard the confessions of those who desired it."[26] In so doing, Claver made public space a performance of the antiblackness supremacist social order.

But Claver did not simply seek to enforce the law. Like all slave masters in relation to their slaves, he was the law. Or, at least, he believed himself to be as much. In this way, Claver sought to punish the city's blacks for behavior that was not even illegal, such as the drinking of a type of sugarcane liquor known as *guarapo*. Claver considered

22. Slattery, *Life of St. Peter Claver,* 147.
23. Splendiani and Aristizabal, *Proceso de beatificación,* 132. My translation.
24. Ibid.
25. Ibid., 133. My translation.
26. Ibid. My translation.

himself the authoritative arbiter of which mind-altering substances black people could ingest: he granted them pinches of snuff as a gift but forbade them the right to manufacture and ingest alcohol.[27] When he could not personally make the city's blacks submit to his will, Claver could marshal the power of the state to do this task on his behalf. For example, he once convinced a high-ranking civil official to prevent the city's blacks from drinking homebrewed alcohol, even though this activity was completely legal.[28] When Claver heard that this official had executed his will, Claver "celebrated mass for [him]."[29] Claver seems quite powerful, even relative to other relatively powerful white men.

Inattention to Claver's historical context may cause us to underestimate the racially evil character of Claver's anti-alcohol crusade. The city's black population made alcohol from scratch at least partially because a late sixteenth-century order of the Cartagena city council had declared it illegal to sell alcohol to slaves. More than simply bringing black people together, alcohol seemed to make them more unruly. This appeared especially the case during funeral celebrations. To the discomfort of many whites, the city's black population would mourn the death of loved ones for several days, wailing, crying, and ingesting large amounts of liquor—all in public.[30] In preventing black people from home-brewing alcohol, Claver did not simply deprive them of a means of relaxation or recreation—he also interfered with their ability to grieve their dead. In this he appears to suppress black fugitivity and rebellion. As the historian Jane Landers explains, alcohol prohibition "reflected an obsession with controlling slave mobility, crime, and marronage."[31]

White Colombians had good reason to be afraid. Demographically and culturally, Claver's Cartagena qualified as one of the largest African cities in the Americas: more than three-fourths of the city's occupants

27. Ibid., 197.
28. Ibid., 198.
29. Ibid. My translation.
30. Pablo Fernando Gómez Zuluaga, *Bodies of Encounter: Health, Illness, and Death in the Early Modern African-Spanish Caribbean* (PhD diss., Vanderbilt University, 2010), 107.
31. Jorge Canizares-Esguerra, Matt D. Childs, and James Sidbury, *The Black Urban Atlantic in the Age of the Slave Trade* (Philadelphia: University of Pennsylvania Press, 2013), 151.

possessed visible African ancestry. In practice if not in Spanish ruling class myth, transplanted African cultural practices existed alongside and sometimes even mingled with those performed by white Spaniards.

The white residents of Cartagena therefore rightly feared any unsupervised massing of blacks, not just those dedicated to mourning the dead. Spanish authorities knew that black people used the fraternal organizations known as *cabilados* not just to "have dances and celebrations after the custom of their African communities" but also "to organize themselves, sometimes [even] to plan rebellions and escapes."[32] In response, "a city governor banned all *cabildo* activity [because of this] fear of rebellion" and white church authorities in Cartagena strove to "confiscate the *cabildos'* drums."[33]

We cannot excuse Claver's campaign against black alcohol consumption or his violent policing of black public gatherings as expressions of misguided but ultimately understandable religious fervor only. In seventeenth century Cartagena, religious opposition to African cultural practices was a political act just as political opposition to African cultural practices was a religious act. We ought to avoid projecting post-Enlightenment conceptions about church-state relations back onto Claver and his contemporaries. Separation of church and state had not sequestered the spiritual in some narrowly privatized and politically neutral sphere. Like many of the city's power brokers, Claver believed the following: Cartagena could not be Spanish if it were not publicly Catholic, and Cartagena could not be Catholic if it were not publicly Spanish, that is, white. For this reason, he did not prohibit African religious practices while permitting the merely cultural ones. No, he deemed all public displays of African culture demonic, regardless of whether they actually contradicted Catholic doctrine. Claver would not have classified the slaves' drums as demonic solely because they deviated from Spanish conventions of religious

32. Peter Wade, *Blackness and Race Mixture: The Dynamics of Racial Identity in Colombia* (Baltimore: Johns Hopkins University Press, 1995), 88.
33. Ibid., 89.

expression; he would have despised them also for their connection to slave rebellion.

Admittedly, we cannot know to what extent Claver modified the public behavior of the city's blacks; even less can we know whether he actually thwarted even a single act of coordinated mass resistance. But we can make assumptions about the reasons that so many segments of the city's population revered and adored him: in confiscating drums and violently dispersing mass gatherings of slaves, Claver did not simply keep black people in their place; he also helped to preserve Cartagena as a white place—in myth if not in reality.[34] In so doing, he operates a saint of antiblackness supremacist order.

4.2 Claver as Overseer of the Spiritual Realm

More than just a master of all the city's slaves, Claver also acted as a type of pacifying overseer of them. As an overseer, Claver also kept unhappy slaves from running away from their masters; he also reconciled these slaves to their masters after they had fled.[35] In so doing, he prevented them from joining the ranks of the women and men who lived in the *palenques* that posed a threat to the city's survival as a citadel of white supremacy. Evidencing this, twentieth century Jesuit William Markoe tells the story of "a girl, driven to desperation by the cruel treatment she had received at the hands of her mistress, resolved to run away and hide in the mountains." She would not have been the first Colombian slave to flee to the mountains in fear of her life. Perhaps, like another seventeenth-century Colombian slave, a woman named Mariana Mandinga, the girl who came to Claver had run away after receiving a beating so ferocious "that she couldn't stir or even stand."[36] Perhaps, like an enslaved woman known as Susana, she escaped after "receiving so many lashes to her buttocks [from her mistress] that the open wounds never ceased to pain her."[37] Or maybe,

34. Splendiani and Aristizabal, *Proceso de beatificación*, 191, 196.
35. Markoe, *Slave of the Negroes*, 35.
36. Block, *Ordinary Lives*, 20.
37. Ibid., 19.

like another enslaved woman named Isabel, she feared that she would be the fifth slave to be whipped to death by her mistress.[38]

Even if Claver did not know the precise details of this girl's suffering, her victimization was unmistakable. When she "came to Father Claver" purportedly "to obtain his blessing" for her flight, her wounds were likely still fresh and noticeable. Despite this, rather than affirming her desire for freedom, Claver "gently pointed out to her the foolhardiness of her plan, which could only lead to her eternal ruin." Undeterred by the knowledge that slave masters and mistresses killed their slaves with impunity, Claver "then kindly persuaded her to accompany him and led her home again."[39] We cannot blame Claver's actions on any fear of imprisonment or civil penalty. He was unbound by a fugitive-slave law such as the one that existed in the United States, which commanded whites to return slaves to their masters no matter the reason they had run away. His society's laws, in fact, granted Claver the option of helping these slaves remain outside the mastery of their abusers.

We may further misread this anecdote by interpreting it as evidence that enslaved people considered Claver a safe haven. In light of the fact that city officials possessed the "power over slaveholders . . . to do what was necessary to penalize the excessively cruel master by selling his slaves" away from him, I suspect that this unnamed slave girl likely visited Claver not to receive his approval but to convince him to represent her case to the secular authorities.[40] This girl likely recognized that Claver's testimony to the authorities would be more credible than her own. She perhaps confessed that her master's abuse had implanted in her the temptation to run away as a ruse rather than as an expression of genuine remorse. Knowing that Claver believed marronage a mortal sin, she perhaps hoped that he would rather arrange for her to be sold away to another master rather than return her to a situation that placed her eternal salvation at risk.

She framed her appeal to be sold as a matter of spiritual need for

38. Ibid., 21.
39. Markoe, *Slave of the Negroes*, 35–36.
40. Block, *Ordinary Lives*, 23.

another reason as well. Like all slave masters, Claver believed that enslaved people had many duties to their masters but few, if any, rights in relation to them. This ideology further encouraged slave masters to imagine themselves as kind benefactors to their chattel: when enslaved people received anything from their masters, they should express gratitude. After all, they had been given something they did not deserve: life. In begging him to arrange for her sale, this girl intelligently flattered Claver's racialized ego: she portrayed herself as dependent upon Claver's intercession but not necessarily worthy of it.

Although the unnamed girl failed to achieve her goal—Claver decided to save her soul not by removing her from her master but returning her to him—she nonetheless acted wisely. According to the hagiographical record, Claver did sometimes convince masters to sell their slaves if they could not treat them "kindly," but he never did so in response to a request made by a slave. Claver refused to allow slaves to exercise even minimal mastery over their own lives. Rendered to a state of unnatural dependence, they were allowed to experience Claver's kindness only as a gift. Enslaved people received his intercessory protection only if he willed it.

A story from the hagiography written by Slattery further establishes Claver's role as overseer. According to him, there once was "an obstinate and scandalous Negro, who heeded neither [Claver's] advice nor his threats." Soon after, this man went missing, "and as a party of Negroes were searching for him they met an enormous crocodile which they killed, and found within, the head and some of the limbs of this unhappy slave." Both Slattery and the search party interpreted this as "conclusive proof" that he had been punished for running away. This event, Slattery recorded, "produced such terror throughout the settlement, that the most hardened began to dread the Divine Justice."[41] Like all overseers, Claver was able to inflict decisive violence against slaves with impunity so as to terrorize them into submission or, at least, to minimize their willingness and ability to resist. It does not matter if this event never occurred: precisely because Claver left

41. Slattery, *Life of St. Peter Claver*, 144.

no written account of his ministerial activities, this story entered the hagiographical record only because it was remembered by a critical mass of people. Even if Claver the historical figure did not terrorize enslaved people in this way, his saintly legend surely did.

Claver turned even the sacrament of marriage into an instrument of pacification. At the beginning of his ministry, many area slave masters believed that Claver in general and the sacrament of marriage in particular would make "the Negroes less serviceable." For this reason, many slave masters barred Claver from ministering to and on their property. But in time Claver more than allayed their fears: "Frequently . . . those masters became convinced by their own experience that under Father Claver's guidance their Negroes were daily more docile and industrious." Grateful for Claver's assistance, these white masters "ultimately left [their slaves] entirely to him."[42] These slave owners considered Claver not a nuisance but their great ally.

Claver's managerial power operated through another sacrament, reconciliation. Enforcing a white-supremacist schema of virtue and vice, Claver classified marronage as a sin. Even post-abolitionist hagiographers such as Slattery praised Claver for his purported capacity to "read the hearts of Negroes who confessed to him, reminding them of the sins which they either had forgotten, or concealed through shame" and to "discover their dissensions, secret enmities, or plans of escape, in spite of their endeavors to hide them." Searching for signs of incipient insubordination, Claver sought not just to remedy sin but also to prevent it. Slattery marveled at "how many [slaves] he was thus enabled to keep to their duty."[43] Claver policed not just the bodies but also the consciences of the black women and men he helped to enslave.

Even Claver's miraculous ability to bring black slaves back from the brink of death serves the interests of slavery. According to Slattery, Claver once revived a slave "who was at the point of death." More than simply reporting about an event that happened to an enslaved person,

42. Bertrand Gabriel Fleuriau, *The Life of the Venerable Father Claver, S.J., Apostle of the West Indies; and Memoirs of the Religious Life of Cardinal Odescalchi, S.J.* (London: Richardson, 1849), 222.
43. Slattery, *Life of St. Peter Claver*, 164.

Slattery's hagiography helps to enslave her. Positioning her as a slave within the text itself, Slattery explains that because this woman was her mistress's "only servant . . . the loss would be irreparable." For Slattery as well as the slave society in which she lived, this woman's value lies primarily and perhaps even exclusively in her relation to her white mistress; in society as well as in Claver's hagiographical afterlife, she exists only through and for her mistress. Thanks to Claver, this woman would live to serve another day: the panicked mistress sent for Father Claver, who arrived and, "after hearing her confession and absolving her . . . said, 'Arise, Mary, and wait upon your mistress!'" According to Slattery, the ailing enslaved woman "obeyed [Claver's command] and from that moment was able to do her usual work."[44] As read through Slattery's hagiography, Claver's sainthood portrays black people as worthy of life only when they obey white people in general and Claver in particular. In this way, for example, when black slaves disobey Claver, they suffer death, in either hell or the jaws of a crocodile; when they obey him, they find new life. But black people continue living only if they remain in a state of social death. In returning this enslaved woman to life, Claver also breathed new life into her enslavement.

44. Ibid., 156.

5

———

Coercive Kindness: Reconsidering Claver "from Below"

How did the Catholic Church end up promoting Claver's sainthood, despite its anti-racist intentions? Claver's baptismal ministry has appeared exceptionally benevolent to so many Catholics largely because the church generally remembers its past through a white-supremacist lens, that is, one that underestimates both the viciousness and the pervasiveness of racialized power in history and contemporary reality. The church similarly has inherited the story of Claver's memory from predecessors who imbibed antiblackness supremacy. This epistemological orientation reflects less the intentions of individual Catholics than the habituating power of the antiblackness supremacist structures that continue to shape the world.[1]

In order to perceive Claver more accurately, the church ought to adopt a new epistemology of memory and remember itself not from the acceptable inside but from the margins. Putting this epistemology

---

1. Jon Sobrino, *Jesus the Liberator: A Historical-Theological Reading of Jesus of Nazareth*, trans. Paul Burns and Francis McDonagh (Maryknoll, NY: Orbis, 1994), 259.

into practice, I present an imaginative but informed reconstruction of the story of Claver's life. I then consider this narrative from the perspective of the slaves to whom he ministered, as suggested by the following sources: scholarship on the slave trade, the few auto-biographies written by formerly enslaved people who survived the Middle Passage, and the hidden transcripts left behind by the witnesses who testified at his beatification proceedings.[2]

This task is perilous. Even where we possess a record of the words of Claver's African contemporaries, we cannot be sure they speak to us in their own voice. Their words undoubtedly are filtered through the prism of white power: they provide answers to questions asked by whites, they participate in a process governed and initiated by white people, and they testify under the shadow of white power. Of the thirty-five black women and men who testified at Claver's beatification proceedings, twenty-four of them were slaves of the Jesuit College, the city hospital, or white residents of Cartagena.[3] Six of these people—Andrés Sacabuche de Angola, Ignacio Alvañil de Angola, Ignacio Soso de los Rios, Francisco Yolofo de los Rios, Manuel Biafra de los Rios, and José Monzolo de los Rios—had been Claver's slaves.[4] In his report about Claver's holiness, the protector of the faith recognized the compromised character of these men's testimony: he doubted whether a slave, intimately indebted to his master, could speak truthfully about that master.[5]

Despite their enslavement to him, Claver's assistants did not simply repeat the words of white witnesses. They actively participated in the process of writing Claver's biography, adding subtle but significant details not found in the testimony of white witnesses. Considering

---

2. Here I again take inspiration from George Tinker, who points out that, in the case of the Jesuit Pierre-Jean De Smet's baptismal ministry to Micmac Indians, it is quite possible that "the baptized Micmacs had no understanding whatsoever of the traditional European Christian significance of the rite but had interpreted it quite differently and within their own cultural frame of reference" (Tinker, *Missionary Conquest*, 14).

3. Nicole von Germeten, "The Problems and Challenges of Research and Writing on Africans and Their Descendants in Colonial Cartagena de Indies: A Research Report," Center for Africana Studies Working Paper Series, no. 002, Johns Hopkins University, http://tinyurl.com/zx4t4mq, 12, 15.

4. Splendiani and Aristizábal, *Proceso de beatificación*, 88.

5. Ibid., 542.

these details as historically credible, I read the testimony of these slaves through what I call "a criterion of punishment." Much as biblical scholars deploy a "criterion of embarrassment" to distinguish historical truth from theological theory, my criterion makes special note of those moments when slave witnesses included a detail not found in anyone else's testimony, especially when this information portrayed Claver unflatteringly. Both because they deviate from the official script and because it places slaves at risk of punishment, these stories of cruelty and violence ought to inhabit an epistemologically privileged position in the church's corporate memory of Claver.

Aiming to challenge the holiness of a man whom we primarily remember through narrative, the counternarrative offered in this chapter must mirror the drama and detail of Claverian hagiographies. It can be neither cursory nor emotionless. This critique attempts to strike what is perhaps an impossible balancing act. It must convince its audience of a truly incredible claim—that the Catholic Church has canonized a violent and cruel man—without reinforcing what Saidiya Hartman terms "the spectacular character of black suffering." As Hartman points out, "Rather than inciting indignation," these descriptions "too often . . . immure us to pain by virtue of their familiarity."[6] While Hartman does include graphic and detailed accounts of horrific suffering in her work, she also attempts to "illuminate the terror of the mundane and quotidian" in order to avoid "exploiting the shocking spectacle."[7] Informed by Hartman's approach, this chapter "invokes the shocking and terrible" aspects of Claver's ministry strategically rather than self-indulgently.[8] Given that most white Catholics continue to perceive both the church and the world through a white-supremacist lens, this chapter must present incontrovertible evidence of Claver's injustice. But this chapter shocks the reader as a means to a greater end. Rather than encouraging the perception that we should reevaluate Claver's sainthood only because of his most violent and grotesque actions, I aim to uncover Claver's

6. Hartman, *Scenes of Subjection*, 3.
7. For an example of the former, see Hartman, *Lose Your Mother*, 120; Hartman, *Scenes of Subjection*, 4.
8. Hartman, *Scenes of Subjection*, 4.

ministry, like slavery itself, as aligned with evil precisely and perhaps especially when he appeared to be kind, loving, and nonviolent.

In embarking upon this imaginative endeavor, I face another danger. As a white woman, I risk a type of minstrelsy wherein I act like a ventriloquist, manipulating the black body like a puppet and making it say whatever I want it to.[9] Indeed, this risk is great. I can never stand outside of my whiteness; I ought never be the final judge of my attempts to oppose white-supremacist forms of embodiment. Even as Claver's hagiographies ought to be read with a hermeneutic of suspicion, so ought my work as well. Indeed, my attempt to examine Claver from the imagined perspective of one of his African subjects admittedly provides not the definitive account of what happened in the slave ships, slave warehouses, and plazas of Cartagena, but a plausible one. This counternarrative qualifies as at least as likely as, if not more so than, the interpreted memories provided by Claver's admirers. It calls attention to the instability and subjectivity of collective memory, encouraging scholars to interrogate their own criteria for credibility. Such interrogations assist in undermining the largely unchallenged authority of white-supremacist structures of memory.

5.1 Stolen Away: Kidnapping, Deception, and Dislocation

Let us outline the hagiographical script this epistemology seeks to interrupt. Witnesses testifying at his beatification hearing recall Claver's baptizing hundreds of thousands of the city's newly arrived Africans; they celebrated his paternal devotion to them: his caressing their diseased and beaten-down bodies, kissing their oozing wounds, hearing their confessions, teaching them the tenets of the Catholic faith, and bringing them gifts of food.[10] They fondly remembered the way he reassured newly arrived Africans that "the Spanish did not bring them to his country in order to eat them nor to make butter of

9. For more on the history of blackface minstrelsy in my U.S.-American context, see Eric Lott, *Love and Theft: Blackface Minstrelsy and the American Working Class* (New York: Oxford University Press, 1993).
10. Splendiani and Aristizábal, *Proceso de beatificación*, 96, 103, 133, 261.

them."[11] Nineteenth- and twentieth-century hagiographers accept this depiction, invariably describing Claver as driven by superhuman love for the enslaved black women and men of Cartagena.[12]

But because we misunderstand the way slavery operates as a violently enforced relation of perverse intimacy, we fail to appreciate the coercive and cruel character of Claver's kindness. Rather than protesting slavery, these acts of kindness comprised essential features of the slave-making system. His ostensibly affectionate relationship with the slaves of Cartagena similarly positions Claver as not a father but a type of slave catcher and master. Unaware of the insidious ways that slavery binds the enslaved to her master, we continue to take Claver's kindness out of context. In order to fully grasp the coercive character of Claver's kindness that was ecclesially expressed in his baptismal ministry, we ought to begin not on the docks of Cartagena but in the towns and villages of Western and Central Africa. Here, we can perceive how integral the interplay of holding captive and displaying kindness proves to the slave-making system.

Remember that the enslaved women and men whom Claver claimed as his children came under his care only by being kidnapped and crammed into the fetid hulls of slave ships. Consider how capture interrupted the seventeenth-century childhood of Ottobah Cugoano, who would survive the Middle Passage and write the story of his life. He begins his tale with an account of a childhood visit to his father, who, in accordance with the matrilineal traditions of the Fante people, "lived at a considerable distance from" young Cugoano's home. There, he passed happy months with "the children of [his] uncle's hundreds of relations," venturing together "into the woods to gather fruit and catch birds."[13] But this happy routine would be cut short. One day,

---

11. Ibid., 113. My translation.
12. See, for example, Brioschi, *Vida de San Pedro Claver*, 96; Valtierra, *Peter Claver*; and Markoe, *Slave of the Negroes*, 56.
13. Ottobah Cugoano, *Thoughts and Sentiments on the Evil and Wicked Traffic of the Slavery and Commerce of the Human Species, Humbly Submitted to the Inhabitants of Great-Britain, by Ottobah Cugoano* (London, 1787), 6. Anthony Bogues argues that we should read this text as not just an autobiography but also as "a major late eighteenth-century text of political discourse on natural liberty and natural rights" ("The Political Thought of Quobna Cugoano: Radicalized Natural Liberty," in *Black Heretics, Black Prophets: Radical Political Intellectuals* [New York: Routledge, 2003], 26).

"several ruffians came upon [them] suddenly," intruding upon their play. Although some of his friends "attempted in vain to run away . . . pistols and cutlasses were soon introduced, threatening, that if [they] offered to stir, [they] should all lie dead on the spot."[14]

Like Claver, these captors used not just violence but also kindness to impress their power upon the children they had taken. Also, like Claver, they promised that they would lead their captives to salvation. Cugoano remembers "one of [the ruffians who] pretended to be more friendly than the rest," assuring them "that he would speak to their lord in order to get us clear, and desired that we should follow him." When they arrived in the town in which this great man allegedly resided, the captors "pretended it was too late to go and see him that night." The next day, a new set of men came to watch them, explaining to Cugoano and his former playmates that they "must put off seeing the great man till after."[15] The captured children believed these men's story; according to Cugoano, they did not imagine "that [their] doom was so nigh, or that these villains meant to feast on [them] as prey."[16] On they traveled for several days, at each stage being reassured that the visit with their lords was still forthcoming.[17]

Other slave traders deployed a strategic mix of violence and kindness to transport their captors to the slave ship. Consider the techniques of eighteenth-century Carolinian slave trader Joseph Hawkins. After restraining his captives "with poles tied around their necks for the march to the river" that would eventually bring them to the sea, he would "calm them [by] promising that such treatment was intended only to keep them from running away." Like Claver, he framed their captivity as for their own good. More than simply protecting them, Hawkins vowed to save them by "taking them to a place where they would be free of their bonds and have complete liberty."[18] This story, at best, could convince only temporarily. Hawkins

14. Cugoano, *Thoughts and Sentiments*, 7.
15. Ibid.
16. Ibid.
17. Ibid., 8.
18. Eric Robert Taylor, *If We Must Die: Shipboard Insurrections in the Era of the Atlantic Slave Trade* (Baton Rouge: Louisiana State University Press, 2006), 15.

then would "order that [the captives] be given alcohol" as a means of pacifying them.[19] Reciting an ideology of slave mastership, Hawkins echoed Claver by characterizing submission as the path to emancipation.

But the promises of both Hawkins and the men who kidnapped Cugoano, of course, were false. Captivity did not lead to freedom. After being marched or shipped in these ways from Africa's interior to its distant coastline, trafficked Africans like Cugoano would be thrown into the dungeons that sat underneath slave fortresses, where they would remain until the next slave ship pulled into view. Although he could not fully describe "the horrors he soon saw and felt" on his way there, Cugoano could recall seeing "many of my miserable countrymen chained two and two." Some were "hand-cuffed" while others came "with their hands tied behind" their backs. Soon, Cugoano went from horrified spectator to terrorized captive: while approaching the coastal slave castle in which he would be imprisoned, a guard told him that he had been brought there in order "to learn the ways of the . . . white faced people."[20]

Once inside these dungeons, captives such as Cugoano could not know when their confinement would end. Tethered to the rhythm of the slave trade, they remained underground for anywhere from a few days to several months. As Saidiya Hartman details, "Sometimes the rooms were packed with as many as fifteen hundred men and boys." Rendered like a living corpse, "each slave was confined to his own place and prevented from moving about the dungeon." Unable to leave even to urinate or defecate, "they ingested and eliminated in the same quarters" as "excrement and food debris accumulated on the floor and soiled their limbs." These conditions, too, bred death. Called the bloody flux by "traders and surgeons . . . because of the profuse discharge of blood, mucus, and pus that were its symptoms," dysentery killed more of these captives than any other ailment.[21]

19. Ibid.
20. Cugoano, *Thoughts and Sentiments*, 9.
21. Hartman, *Lose Your Mother*, 120.

5.2 From Life to Death: Hell on the High Seas

But the ship's often long-awaited arrival did not bring relief. Those who refused to board the ship "were lashed and beat in the most horrible manner."[22] As Cugoano reported, when "a vessel arrived to conduct us away to the ship, it was a most horrible scene. There was to be heard but rattling of chains, smacking of whips, and the groans and cries of our fellow-men." The loading process could take days, or even months, depending upon the speed at which human cargo was arriving to the coast.[23] A slave ship would not depart until it was full. Many enslaved women and men therefore languished on board in a state of immeasurable suspension for months.[24]

In a way, slaves such as Cugoano already had suffered death: "lost to [his] dear indulgent parents and relations, and they to [him]," he had been natally alienated and therefore rendered socially dead.[25] According to Cugoano, natal alienation in particular made enslaved women and men desire to be physically dead as well. Cugoano recounts how "when we found ourselves at last taken away [from the shore], death was more preferable than life, and a plan was concerted amongst us, that we might burn and blow up the ship, and to perish all together in the flames." The plot was discovered before it could be enacted: when the white masters of the ship heard word of the plot, Cugoano describes "the discovery [as] a cruel bloody scene."[26]

Women and men pursued other methods of self-emancipation. A white passenger on another slave-ship reported "that when a large gust of wind pushed a vessel over on its side, the slaves would sometimes all together rush to the low side with the intent of capsizing the ship."[27] In order to prevent this, slave-ship captains would shackle the slaves to the ship and subject them to constant surveillance. On other occasions, slaves would resist their living death by refusing to

22. Cugoano, *Thoughts and Sentiments*, 9.
23. Taylor, *If We Must Die*, 19.
24. Spillers, "Mama's Baby, Papa's Maybe," 210.
25. Cugoano, *Thoughts and Sentiments*, 10.
26. Ibid.
27. Taylor, *If We Must Die*, 38.

eat the food placed before them. In so doing, they also unsettled a social order organized according to white power and authority.[28] Slave traders possessed a perverse relation to the lives of the enslaved: they forced them to stay alive so that they could keep them in a state of social death.

Other enslaved women and men decided not to die but to kill. Mutinies sometimes proved successful. For this reason, slave traders shared with each other trusted methods of management and pacification in order to lessen the risk of insurrection. The early eighteenth-century French navigator Chevalier des Marchais, one of the leading experts on this subject, sounded much like Claver when he insisted that "treating the captives with 'humanity' and 'tenderness' would keep them from rebelling." As if quoting Claver directly, he maintained that it was even more important "to tell the captives through an interpreter that they were not going to be eaten by white cannibals; rather, they were being taken to till the soil for white masters in a faraway country."[29] So another slave trader advised his colleagues to prevent mutiny by "giving the slaves occasional gifts of tobacco and brandy."[30]

5.3 The Violent Cruelty of Claver's Kindness

Let us now imagine Claver's ministry from the perspective of one who experienced these particular horrors.[31] When Claver "went through the streets of the city . . . obtaining from charitable persons a large supply of biscuits, preserves, brandy, [and] tobacco," which he would give to slaves upon their arrival, would he not have resembled the notorious Anglo-American slave catcher Hawkins?[32] These drugs undoubtedly made his subjects more pliable. Like the aforementioned slave traders, Claver wished to appease them in order to draw them

---

28. Marcus Rediker, *The Slave Ship: A Human History* (New York: Penguin, 2008), 288.
29. Robert Harms, *The Diligent: A Voyage through the Worlds of the Slave Trade* (New York: Basic Books, 2002), 271.
30. Ibid., 300.
31. As Tinker contends, "Language and behavior must be understood in terms of people's experiences of the world" (Tinker, *Missionary Conquest*, 34).
32. Markoe, *Slave of the Negroes*, 23.

more deeply into a perverse and dehumanizing form of belonging. If we find this judgment too harsh, it is only because our history has rendered slavery more mundane and therefore more forgivable than it really is. In order to step outside our antiblackness-supremacist context, let us judge Claver as we would any of our contemporaries who received a trafficked person: would we deem the candy given by modern kidnappers to be sweet?

As Cugoano's narrative reveals, for many newly arrived Africans, Claver would not have been the first person to pose as their friend, ally, and savior. They would have learned that the promises of white men were not to be trusted. Disoriented, dislocated, and rendered completely dependent, these women and men had been deprived of any reliable frame of reference with which to discern credible whites from dishonest ones. Even if Claver did not appear to them like just another captor, they at least would have recognized the great power he held over them and would have understood the perils of disobeying or upsetting him.

Claver likely resembled their kidnappers in yet another way. As on the slave ship, some slaves continued to resist their enslavement by refusing to eat even after arriving at Cartagena. One white witness at Claver's beatification proceedings recalled, "On some occasions . . . there were some blacks from the slave ship who were sick [or] who did not want to eat because they were furious or almost desperate upon seeing themselves away from their home lands." Ultimately, he explained, "they wanted . . . to die of hunger."[33] Claver would convince them to eat by "showing them a picture of hell that he had brought with him, which showed a soul in hell who was very ugly . . . and was suffering" intensely. Those who obeyed him by eating, he explained, would go to heaven while those who disobeyed by refusing his food would languish in hell. Upon seeing these pictures and hearing his words, the slaves would then eat.[34] Claver's hagiographers describe this act as a source of great comfort to the city's enslaved Africans.[35] But is

33. Splendiani and Aristizábal, *Proceso de beatificación*, 214. My translation.
34. Ibid., 215.
35. See, for example, Slattery, *Life of St. Peter Claver*, 57.

this true? In order to answer this question, we must consider the ways in which food had been used against slaves during the Middle Passage. When the crews of slave ships could not convince recalcitrant slaves to eat, they would physically force food down their throats using one of a variety of violent techniques.[36] Knowing that many of them had been physically forced to eat, we wonder whether these women and men would have believed themselves able to refuse Claver's offer.

More than simply ensuring that they ate, Claver also assuaged their fear that they were brought to Cartagena in order to be eaten. But even this kindness served the ends of slaveocracy. In so doing, Claver helped to pacify these intransigent newcomers, neutralizing the threat they would otherwise pose to the civic order.[37] Slave owners throughout the Americas understood the inherently dangerous character of slavery: more slaves meant not just more power but an increased risk of insurrection. Whites especially feared so-called *bozales*, those African-born women and men who they believed still carried the uncivilized savagery of Africa within their bodies. The slave docks and warehouses of Cartagena remained outside the city's walls: wild Africans must be tamed before they could be allowed inside the city.[38] Claver's gifting black slaves with food occupies a prominent role in hagiographical narratives about him because of its perceived powers of slave pacification.[39] Through his baptismal ministry, Claver turned potentially pathogenic invaders into food that the city's social body could consume. Claver turned dangerous *bozales* into docile children of white fathers, even if only in the imaginations of those elite whites who would exalt Claver as a symbol of civic order.[40]

Claver's helping to transport sick slaves from slave ship to holding pen as well as his catechizing slaves there also comprise his hagiographical renown.[41] But, when considered from the perspective

---

36. Taylor, *If We Must Die*, 37.
37. Markoe, *Slave of the Negroes*, 55–56.
38. Linda A. Newson, *From Capture to Sale: The Portuguese Slave Trade to Spanish South America in the Early Seventeenth Century* (Leiden: Brill, 2007), 144–45; Block, "Faith and Fortune," 24.
39. Block, "Faith and Fortune," 24. See, for example, Brioschi, *Vida de San Pedro Claver*, 95.
40. Ibid., 153–54.
41. Ibid., 114.

of an enslaved African child, woman, or man, these actions appear not saintly but sinister. Just a few days away from the Middle Passage, these human beings undoubtedly would have been in a state of tremendous fear and anxiety. During this time, they also would have endured mistreatment by slave merchants, who would routinely "parade [them] through the streets of Cartagena" in order to whet the appetites of potential buyers. Precisely because it humiliated those made to participate in it, these processions also delighted and amused the many white onlookers who celebrated them as a type of festival.[42] Captured women and men therefore experienced Claver's catechesis during this period of humiliation, confinement, and uncertainty.

Amplifying their anxiety, in these warehouses, Claver again used images of hell to compel them to accept baptism. According to Sacabuche, Claver "taught them the immortality of the souls and how there was hell for the evil and heaven for the good and that if they weren't Christian they would go to not heaven but hell in which there was fire' and tremendous suffering."[43] To his captive audience, Claver's homilies about hell and salvation likely would have sounded not persuasive, as Claver's hagiographers claim, but terrifying. Rendered perversely and artificially dependent upon the will and power of whites, the Middle Passage had taught them that they lived only if and in the manner in which whites permitted. These evangelizing images suggested that this would hold true even in the afterlife. They could disobey Claver and remain trapped in everlasting death, or they could accede to his will and be spared eternal torment. One imagines that this news filled many slaves with unbearable dread and panic: if their soul would live in the lands of the whites forever, then not even death could set them free. Their experience of the Middle Passage surely convinced these women and men that white people were both willing and able to lock them in hell. They had already died and gone to hell once; could not white people send them there a second time?

Attending more closely to Claver's historical context makes this

42. Zuluaga, "Bodies of Encounter," 42.
43. Splendiani and Aristizabal, *Proceso de beatificación*, 102. My translation.

interpretation more likely, not less so. Many of the Africans Claver coercively baptized came from cultures in which both the afterlife as well as those who resided there would have looked quite similar to the world they encountered on the slave ship and after its arrival at New Granada. According to the cosmology that predominated in West Central Africa, in the afterlife, "the dead moved around in the same shape as they had on earth, but whitened like the clay of a riverbed." So they imagined the land of the dead as separated from the land of the living that it mirrored "by a large body of water—an ocean or a great river—and death itself was an extended journey which took a certain length of time." It is quite possible that these people thought they were literally in a hellish afterlife.[44]

Claver's acts of kindness also were quite cruel. Instructing slaves in the rules of submission, Claver repeatedly dramatized the terms of their enslavement: those who obeyed and expressed gratitude received treats and a break from the lash; those who disobeyed and expressed discontent would be hit, beaten, and deprived of even simple pleasures.[45] Like slave masters everywhere, Claver inflicted pain or allowed pleasure in order to engineer submission. Conditioned into submission, these slaves already knew they could not disobey white men like Claver without suffering a beating or worse. Claver's deployment of disciplining violence rendered it even more unlikely that slaves would have believed him to be any different from the dozens, if not hundreds, of men with whips, pistols, chains, and ropes whose wrath they had felt during their journey to Cartagena. While Claver may have been kind to the slaves, we cannot say that he was truly good to them.

---

44. Andrew Redden, "The Problem of Witchcraft, Slavery, and Jesuits in Seventeenth-Century New Granada," *Bulletin of Hispanic Studies* 90, no. 2 (2013): 232–33.
45. For example, according to Frederick Douglass, "holidays were among the most effective means in the hands of slave-holders of keeping down the spirit of insurrection among the slaves" (Frederick Douglass and William Lloyd Garrison, *Narrative of the Life of Frederick Douglass, An American Slave* [Boston: The Anti-Slavery Office, 1849], 74).

5.4 Suspicious Transcripts: Speaking Truth Despite Power

For the most part, the *Proceso* provides an exceptionally consistent account of Claver's holiness. Rather than evidencing its credibility, this coherence in fact provides a reason to question it. Pointing out that the text of Claver's *Proceso* quite unusually lacks both "question and answer sessions" and an explanation "as to why many witnesses repeat the same testimony given by González," Germeten suspects that González, the person who initiated the investigation into Claver's sainthood, exercised "an undue influence on the testimonies" included in the *Proceso*.[46] Claver's seven African-descended interpreters, after all, were slaves of the Jesuit college to which González belonged. For this reason, González wielded a particular type of power over them. So did the priestly official of the Inquisition who monitored their testimonies. In addition to speaking under the threat of white violence as all black slaves did, these interpreters answered questions formulated by white minds for the sake of white prerogatives while white notaries captured their words and transformed them into a text.[47]

Despite this, Claver's enslaved interpreters did depart from the narrative provided by González in one significant way. Their testimonies "stress more of the violence in the stories and images" of Claver's ministry, even describing "physical beatings."[48] For example, Claver's slave Ignacio recalls how during the pre-baptismal catechesis Claver conducted in the slave warehouses, "he would use the room key that hung from a rope on his belt to hit on the head those" he deemed insufficiently attentive or who were unable to make the sign of the cross to his satisfaction, for example.[49] Andrés Sacubuche explains that sometimes Claver would deliver this blow with not a key but "the stick of the cross" he carried with him. Like other slave masters, Claver sometimes would delegate disciplining violence to subordinates, commanding his enslaved assistants to deliver these "blows to the

---

46. Germeten, "Problems and Challenges," 12.
47. Zuluaga, "Bodies of Encounter," 127–28.
48. Germeten, "Problems and Challenges," 15.
49. Splendiani and Aristizabal, *Proceso de beatificación*, 106. My translation.

heads" of slow learners.[50] From the perspective of African women and men locked inside the city's sweltering slave warehouses, Claver likely resembled the dozens, if not hundreds, of men with whips, pistols, chains, and ropes whose wrath they had felt during their journey to Cartagena.

This seems even more likely given that for many of Claver's enslaved students, even those who were not already Catholic, this would have been their first encounter with the cross. Slave traders seared the sign of the cross into the right arm of each of these slaves upon their arrival to one of the Portuguese slave fortresses that lined the coast of Africa.[51] The sign they now made with their bodies at the end of the Middle Passage had already been burned into them at its beginning. In catechizing newly arrived Africans in this way, Claver helped to incorporate them into not just Christianity but also the life of enslavement.[52]

Sacabuche includes another aspect of Claver's ministry that González omits. According to Sacabuche, Claver also disciplined enslaved children: for example, "if during Lent he encountered some black children who was playing with a ball . . . he would . . . take the ball away from him." Even more disturbingly, Sacabuche recalls that Claver would visit the homes in which young slaves lived and ask "the owners if they had among them [any black children] who had the custom of swearing or saying bad words." If the white owners said yes, Claver "ordered [the offending enslaved child] to kiss the ground" so that Claver could then "place his foot on [the prostrate slave's] head." Before he left, he would "encourage [a white authority figure] . . . to let him know if the black little boy or girl in question started swearing again."[53]

The willingness of the enslaved interpreters to mention these otherwise forgotten details proves even more remarkable given their

50. Ibid., 101. My translation.
51. Newson, *From Capture to Sale*, 63.
52. While these pedagogical techniques may have been widespread in earlier eras, when deployed in the context of racialized slavery, they become not indicators of cultural diversity but accomplices to enslavement. For this reason, they cannot be excused.
53. Splendiani and Aristizábal, *Proceso de beatificación*, 193. My translation.

status as "elite assistants." Although they suffered true slavery, they still occupied a slightly different relation to Claver's ministerial power than other members of the city's enslaved population. Although I can only speculate at these men's intentions, perceptions, and feelings, it seems likely that they would have perceived Claver's ministry more favorably than many other black women and men. If enslaved men who spoke about Claver under the shadow of white power described him as monstrously violent toward black children, one can only imagine what the city's other slaves said about Claver behind closed doors.

At this point, defenders of Claver might wish to overturn my assessment by pointing to the reported actions of the slaves themselves. According to witnesses at his beatification proceedings, black women and men would kiss Claver's hand while kneeling before him whenever they passed him on the city streets.[54] Claver's white hagiographers in turn cite these accounts as evidence of the love that the city's African-descended inhabitants felt for him. But in making these claims, both the witnesses at the beatification hearings and later hagiographers offer not an objective description of the intentions, actions, and interior lives of Cartagena's slaves but an interpretation of them. The slaves' treatment of Claver much more likely reflects not their respect for him but the power he held over them. Lacking the power to openly defy a white man like Claver, these slaves most likely flattered the sensibilities of their masters as a way of survival.

Powerless groups such as slaves and serfs "are often obliged to adopt a strategic pose in the presence of the powerful."[55] Aiming to "produce a more or less credible performance" before their audience of elites, these populations "speak the lines and make the gestures [they know] are expected of [them]."[56] The autobiographical accounts written by slaves held in other parts of the Americas affirm the near universality of this strategy. A former US-American slave writes,

---

54. Splendiani and Aristizábal, *Proceso de beatificación*, 119. For hagiographical accounts of the black population's affection for Claver, see Brioschi, *Vida de San Pedro Claver*, 226.
55. James C. Scott, *Domination and the Arts of Resistance: Hidden Transcripts* (New Haven, CT: Yale University Press, 1990), xii.
56. Ibid., 4.

I had endeavored so to conduct myself as not to become obnoxious to the white inhabitants, knowing as I did their power, and their hostility to the colored people. . . . First, I had made no display of the little property or money I possessed, but in every way I wore as much as possible the aspect of slavery. Second, I had never appeared to be even so intelligent as I really was. This all colored [in] the south, free and slaves, find it particularly necessary for their own comfort and safety to observe.[57]

Surely many of the slaves of Cartagena would have played this game in their interactions with white men like Claver. In addition to his unchecked power to publicly beat them with impunity, he wielded the authority to convince their masters to sell them away from their new, courageously reconstructed American families, and he could encourage their masters to beat them less savagely if he so desired.[58]

One early twentieth-century hagiographer unwittingly confirms this reading when he writes, "So great was [Claver's] influence among them that one Negro could not utter a severer threat against another than to say he would tell Father Claver" of his misdeeds.[59] When enslaved people ran away from him, they likely did so not because they did not want to be seen offending him but because they feared his power to beat them. Even when the city's slaves did in fact obsequiously kiss and lavish affection upon him, they most likely did so not because they loved and admired him but because they needed to flatter him in order to survive. Put another way, any affection the city's slave population felt for Claver, however sincere, likely represents neither familial love nor Christian virtue but the sentiments of a slave for her master.[60]

In addition to doubting the sincerity of these public performances of black gratitude, we also ought to question the accuracy of the aforementioned white interpretations of black behavior. Above all, socially powerful populations wish to present their rule as being voluntarily, and even gleefully, accepted by those below them.[61] Slave-

57. Ibid., 2.
58. Splendiani and Aristizábal, *Proceso de beatificación*, 195, 328.
59. Markoe, *Slave of the Negroes*, 39.
60. Thus, even if these expressions of adoration were sometimes sincere and authentic, they should still disturb us. They should not be taken as signs of saintliness.
61. Arana, "Pedro Claver y la evangelización en Cartagena," 255.

owning classes in particular pepper the public transcript with euphemisms designed to "mask the many nasty facts of domination and give them a harmless or sanitized aspect."[62] For example, González pointed to the fact that when "black people who were chatting in the city's streets and plazas with a person of the opposite sex would see Claver coming, even from very far away, they would interrupt their conversations and immediately walk away from each other" as evidence of just "how much respect black females and black males of this city had for Father Claver and his Christian fervor."[63] When witnesses who belonged to Cartagena's white elite claimed that black people revered and loved Claver so much that they expressed more intense grief at Claver's death than they had at their separation from their natural parents, we ought to hear these accounts as a type of public transcript that aims to smooth over the sharp and bloody edges of slavery.[64] These descriptions reveal not the truth but the social fantasies of the city's elite. What could secure a slave master's power more than the belief that enslaved people embraced their natal alienation?

But the truth about both slavery and Claver could not be hidden entirely: even the words of those who witnessed to Claver's holiness unwittingly imply that Claver was more terrifying than tender. In this way, González describes how, when Claver encountered a black woman and man conversing, he would take out his *disciplina,* a rod designed for flogging, and beat them with it until they dispersed. It initially may appear as though Claver treated black people no differently than he would either himself or other Jesuits. Indeed, the Jesuits did deploy the so-called "Spanish discipline" as a penitential practice. But the Spanish discipline differed from the beatings Claver administered in both content and symbolic import. First, Jesuits were flagellated only by their confessors. Second, even if they did not always want to be disciplined in this way, their bodies experienced violence only as a result of relationships into which they entered voluntarily.[65] No one

---

62. Scott, *Domination and the Arts of Resistance,* 53.
63. Splendiani and Aristizabál, *Proceso de beatificación,* 190. My translation.
64. Ibid., 119, 317–18.

made them join this order. Third, this penitential practice occurred in private only; Jesuit confessors did not flay their charges in public. The violence Claver inflicted on black people differed even from those sixteenth century lay Spanish Catholics who did scourge themselves in public. These women and men punished themselves voluntarily; they performed not servility, but self-mastery. When Claver whipped black women and men in public, he enacted not their mastery, but his own.[66] Fourth, because women were considered to be too delicate to be whipped by their male confessor, Jesuit custom permitted women to be physically disciplined only by their own hands.[67] But not a single hagiographical source records Claver ever refusing to lash black women. Although this Jesuit protocol may have been founded on an outdated view of women, in beating both sexes equally, Claver treated black women as uniquely unworthy of protection.

Claver's more recent admirers also provide us reason to perceive Claver's disciplining practices as performances of white mastership. Praising Claver's intolerance for black people's "loitering in the streets, wasting their time indulging in useless gossip," Slattery similarly notes that Claver's "appearance was enough to scatter them to their homes."[68] Claver would whip black people caught playing certain games in public and chase after them. He sometimes even ran them down with his horse.[69] Surely this level violence far exceeds that included in existing Jesuit spiritual practices. Interpreted from the underside of Cartagena's history, black people's responses to Claver's lashing express not love or affection for him, but fear and even hatred of him.

Even without these incriminating details, we still ought to read claims that black people were grateful for Claver with suspicion.

65. William M. Cooper, *The History of the Rod: Flagellation and the Flagellants from All Countries from the Earliest Period to the Present Time* (New York: Routledge, 2009), 96–97.
66. Mary Francis Cusack, *The Black Pope: A History of the Jesuits* (London, UK: Marshall, Russell, 1896), 309–13.
67. Haruko Nawata Ward, *Women Religious Leaders in Japan's Christian Century, 1549–1650* (Burlington, VT: Ashgate, 2009), 326
68. Slattery, *Life of St. Peter Claver*, 71.
69. Splendiani and Aristizabál, *Proceso de beatificación*, 191. Arana, "Pedro Claver," 318. Claver did not discipline whites who played games in public.

Gratitude plays a central role in ideologies of slave mastership, which figure the slave as indebted to her master: from his slave, a slave master arguably desires gratitude even more than he seeks obedience. An enslaved person differs from other human beings because she both "had to depend exclusively on a single person for protection" and could neither exercise rights over nor fulfill obligations to other people without her master's permission.[70] For example, because enslaved parents could not claim their children as their own, they could not protect them from their master. Nor could these enslaved parents be protected reliably from the wrath of their master by anyone else. Freedom, then, entails not the lack of obligations but the perfectly dispersed mix of rights and corresponding duties to a community of people.

Thus, even when Claver reportedly would convince white masters to beat their slaves less savagely or when he brought the city's slaves little gifts, he ought not to be perceived as one who defended their dignity or protected them from harm. In performing these little acts of kindness, he situated the city's slaves in a relation of pervasive and dishonorable indebtedness to him. For example, although Claver delighted in bringing black slaves gifts of food and perfume, he violently interrupted black people's ability to buy and sell these same goods on their own terms. González fondly recalls how, if Claver saw "some black male sitting next to one of the black females who were selling groceries" in the city's Plaza de la Yerba, "he would get very disgusted and reprimand him very severely," remaining until the black women and men obeyed him and left the scene.[71]

But he did not oppose intercourse between women and men in all circumstances. Claver encouraged the city's black women to interact with men like his translators and him for the sake of receiving gifts both sacramental and edible. Why? While their commercial encounter with men suggested sexual and economic independence, their contact with Claver and his men placed these women in a state of artificial

70. Patterson, *Slavery and Social Death*, 28.
71. Splendiani and Aristizábal, *Proceso de beatificación*, 190. My translation.

dependence upon him. After dismantling these black women's produce stands, he would confiscate their contents.[72] Enlisting the supervisory help of other white men, Claver would hand these items over to the owner of a nearby store, "telling him that they ought not be returned to the black woman until she pays a real or two in alms for the poor of San Lazaro hospital."[73]

Claver likely believed himself entitled to violently discipline black people this way because he had baptized them. Why? For Claver, the slaves he baptized arrived in a Christian land involuntarily. The enslaved Africans may have appeared to consent to baptism, but they did not make it happen. Claver believed that they were brought to salvation as a result of the actions of their kidnappers.[74] As those who deserved death due to unpardoned original sin but were gifted life that they did not earn, the city's African-born women and men lived not by right but only by his mercy. For this reason, Claver expected slaves still shackled inside the hulls of the slave ships that had stolen them away from their life, land, and loved ones to greet him with pure gratitude.[75]

5.5 Conclusion

More than simply helping to turn certain people into slaves, Claver's ministry helped to turned slavery into a racially exclusive institution. It did so by strengthening the association between blackness and slave status: Claver's sainthood casts black people as simultaneously repulsive yet sexually dangerous, uniquely violent, dependent on and grateful to white saviors, incapable of self-direction and decision-making, stigmatized and contaminating, and moral only when obedient and pacified.[76] Africanized slavery possesses a unique ability to outlive its own abolition. Just as black slaves created wealth for their masters, so the association between blackness and slave status

72. Ibid., 190.
73. Ibid. My translation.
74. Ibid. 93. My translation.
75. Patterson, *Slavery and Social Death*, 5, 26, 224.
76. For more on the way contemporary patterns of antiblackness supremacy label black people as hypersexual and how this expresses the logic of racialized slavery, see Kelly Brown Douglas, *Stand Your Ground: Black Bodies and the Justice of God* (Maryknoll, NY: Orbis, 2015), 64–68.

helped to construct American cultures, financial institutions, political systems, and ethical and political ideals. Although black slavery eventually ended, the worlds it helped to create did not. As long as Claver appears exceptionally virtuous, the collective Catholic imagination will continue to perceive black people as ordinarily incapable of it. As long as he appears to model humility, Catholics will continue to consider black people as worthy of love but only occasionally of justice. As long as it considers Claver a protective father, the Catholic church will continue to misunderstand that white people mistreat black people not so much by pushing them away but holding them in a place.

6

The Racialized Humility of
Saint Martín de Porres

The contextual and critical re-evaluation of Claver's sainthood offered in the preceding section prompts us to re-consider the case of the church's other American racial saint, Martín de Porres. Rather than an isolated error, Claver's hagiographical acclaim unfortunately expresses a corporate vice.[1] Like Claver's, Porres' sainthood has helped to promote, sanction, and excuse white mastership; it similarly has helped to portray black resistance to and fugitivity from white mastership as unholy, unwise, and harmful to society itself. Relying once again on Patterson's definition of slavery, this analysis details why Porres' contemporaries as well as subsequent generations of Catholics have considered him a saint. Rather than self-servingly detaching either Porres or his hagiographers from their respective cultural backgrounds, this analysis places them more securely inside of them.

---

1. For more on the theory of corporate virtue and vice that informs this article, see Katie M. Grimes, "Breaking the Body of Christ: The Sacraments of Initiation in a Habitat of White Supremacy," *Political Theology* (forthcoming).

Which of Porres' contemporaries considered him a saint? White priests belonging to Porres' Dominican order and "a couple of Afroperuvian laymen with ties to the elite also helped to push his case through."[2] Contemporary notions of racial identity may mislead us. We must resist the temptation to interpret the blackness of Porres' early lay champions by the standards of distinctly postabolition U.S. American notions of racial solidarity. In many slave-holding American societies, free people of color did not necessarily side with enslaved blacks in political struggles, nor did they oppose racialized slavery. Although free people of color were treated as racially inferior to white people, they typically sided with their white oppressors in efforts to keep enslaved blacks in their place.[3] After all, a certain group can protest their subordination to the group above them even as they strive to preserve their advantage over the group below them. Porres' Afro-Peruvian supporters were men of their times: to them, they likely accorded tremendous importance to the distinction between black and mulatto.[4]

The racial affiliations of African-descended Peruvians notwithstanding, we do not have to infer the reasons his white fellow Dominican priests and brothers lauded him. Porres's first hagiographers, Bernardo de Medina and Cipriano de Medina, articulate them explicitly. Written thirty six years after Porres' death and fifteen after his first beatification hearing, Bernardo's 1675 work portrayed Porres as both "a humble servant descended from enslaved Africans, and . . . the extremely capable, pious and industrious, albeit illegitimate, son of an elite father."[5] Porres' mulatto status made him an exemplar to blacks and whites alike: his soul represented white

2. Cussen, *Black Saint of the Americas*, 12.
3. See, for example, Laurent DuBois, *Avengers of the New World: The Story of the Haitian Revolution* (Cambridge, MA: Harvard University Press, 2009), 70; and Jared Sexton, *Amalgamation Schemes: Antiblackness and the Critique of Multiculturalism* (Minneapolis: University of Minnesota Press, 2008), 12.
4. For more on the meaning of blackness and mulatez in seventeenth century Peru, see Larissa Brewer-García, "Negro, pero blanco de alma: La ambivalencia de le negrura en la *Vida prodigiosa* de Fray Martín de Porras (1663)," *Cuadernos del CILHA* 13, no. 2 (2012): 113–46. Accessed on December 17, 2016 from http://www.scielo.org.ar/scielo.php?script=sci_arttext&pid=S1852-96152012000 200008&lng=es&tlng=pt.
5. Cussen, *Black Saint of the Americas*, 11.

virtue while his body modelled it for blacks. For this reason, civil and ecclesial authorities promoted his humility as a standard that all Peruvians ought to follow. Rather than undermining racial hierarchy as many of Porres' hagiographers have claimed, his universality in fact helps to uphold it.[6]

Consider the central role that Porres' self-disciplinary practices played in establishing his initial hagiographical renown.[7] According to Cipriano, Porres "was known to have performed physical acts of penance three times a day, scourging different parts of his own body with a chain until blood was drawn, then asking a fellow Dominican to wash his wounds with vinegar." During his beatification hearing, a teenaged boy described as his "helper" recounted "how he reluctantly obliged the saint by whipping him."[8] So Bernardo lauds the way Porres would visit the black slaves held on the Dominican-owned *hacienda* called Limatambo and whip himself bloody in front of them.[9]

As was the case in my assessment of Claver's penitential practices, I do not critique Porres's self-discipline simply because they seem historically foreign or strange to me. They ought to disturb us primarily for the horrifying racial lesson they teach: just as Porres' white soul must beat his rebellious black body in order to keep it at bay and in line, so must whites discipline blacks with similar intensity. I do not put words in his hagiographers' mouths: Bernardo makes this racial connection explicit when he recalls that Porres "treated his body like a rebel slave or mortal enemy."[10] The same action performed by a white man such as Claver means something entirely different when enacted by a mulatto person such as Porres. According to Bernardo, when Porres whipped his own flesh, he modeled what blacks ought to endure and what whites ought to inflict. He appeared to sanctify the

---

6. For examples of this hagiographical defense, see Cussen, *Black Saint of the Americas*, 194; Brewer-García, "Negro, pero blanco de alma."
7. Celia Langdeau Cussen, *Fray Martín de Porres and the religious imagination of Creole Lima* (PhD diss., University of Pennsylvania, 1996), 149.
8. Ibid.
9. Brewer-García, "Negro, pero blanco de alma."
10. Chris Garces, "The Interspecies Logic of Race in Colonial Peru: San Martín de Porres's Animal Brotherhood," in *Sainthood and Race: Marked Flesh, Holy Flesh*, ed. Molly H. Bassett and Vincent W. Lloyd (New York: Routledge, 2014), 96.

racialized master-slave relation in his own body.[11] Bernardo's words contain another truth: implicitly white rebel slaves are the implicitly white master's mortal enemy. Just as the disobedient body would damn the soul to eternal death, so a rebel slave threatens to deprive his master of temporal life.

As in Claver's sainthood, these purely political beliefs carry deep theological consequences. Just as Porres' black body can be made holy only through violent punishment doled out by his white soul, so black people can be turned into Christians only with the assistance of the slave master's lash. Porres' penitential practices suggest that black people were not simply incorporated into the church as slaves; they were incorporated into the church only if they were slaves. Ecclesial inclusion did not protest their enslavement as much as it helped to sustain it.

Consider Bernardo's account of Porres' tendency to visit the Limatambo hacienda and "discipline himself so rigorously" before an audience of black slaves that "rivers full of blood [would] run down his back onto the ground."[12] Indulging in a slave master's ultimate fantasy, Bernardo insisted that these enslaved spectators expressed gratitude to Porres for whipping himself in this way, and proclaimed his practice "a blessed imitation of the Lord."[13] We ought not to trust the words Bernardo placed in the mouths of the slaves who observed this spectacle. Imagine Porres' performance at Limatambo from the perspective of the women, children, and men held captive there. Would not the sight of Porres' mulatto skin ripped open by the lash evoke memories of the beatings that they and their loved ones had received at the hands of kidnappers and masters? It would not matter even if these people did derive some sort of inspiration from Porres' penitential display. Nor would it change our assessment of Porres' sainthood if he interpreted his self-disciplinary regimen differently than his hagiographers. Porres inhabits the church's memory only

11. Brewer-García, "Negro, pero blanco de alma."
12. Ibid., 34. My translation.
13. Ibid.

as a saintly story; we cannot retrieve a historical Porres that exists independently of that.

Porres first hagiographers used his mixed race status to celebrate both the church in general and the Dominican Order in particular. According to Bernardo, for example, black people were not spiritually equal to whites. Porres' parentage proved this. He described Porres' conception as a "bright dawn" that marked the passage from "the dark night" of his enslaved mother's blackness to the enlightened whiteness of his aristocratic father. Due to the victories his white soul won over his black body, Porres himself would "grow to a resplendent sun."[14] Porres' sainthood upholds a racial double standard precisely because he models a holiness that all women and men ought to follow. For Bernardo, Porres' mulatto status symbolizes the transformation that all people experience when they are submerged in the waters of Christian baptism only because it symbolizes the transformation that only black people must achieve. He imagines Christianity itself as a passageway to whiteness.

But of course black people can never acquire white bodies; according to Bernardo, they therefore un-coincidentally struggle to obtain white souls. A conclusion easily follows from this: black people must be placed under the authority of those who are both light and enlightened. More than simply using *mulatez* as a symbol for the ancient Christian metaphor of enlightenment, Bernardo transformed this ancient metaphor into an instrument of racial hierarchy. For Bernardo, Porres also operates as an icon both of Catholic Spain's evangelizing work among black Africans and of the Dominican order's contribution to this endeavor; according to Bernardo, "God used the white and black colors of his parents in order to forecast the habit of Saint Dominick" that he would one day wear.[15] Like Claver's champions, Bernardo believed that white people could serve as slaves to God by acting as masters of blacks while black people could find freedom in God only if they toiled as slaves to white masters.

14. Ibid.; Bernardo de Medina, *Vida prodigiosa del venerable siervo de Dios Fr. Martin de Porras* (Madrid: Domingo Garcia Morrás, 1675), 3–4.
15. Brewer-García, "Negro, pero blanco de alma." My translation.

6.1 Porres as a Balm to White Minds

Despite the explicitly antiblackness supremacist ideology of Porres's first hagiographers, many contemporary Christians still consider him an icon of racial justice. Why? As they do when considering Claver's sainthood, many modern-day Catholics overestimate the anti-racist character of Porres's sainthood in large part because they mistakenly assume the segregationist ethos of Jim Crow to be the essence of antiblackness supremacy rather than a specific version of it.[16] In truth, even Jim Crow used segregation as a mere tactic: white Southerners sought to separate themselves from blacks only when and if it strengthened slavery's afterlife. Guided by this misapprehension, the fact that Porres' loved and was loved by people of all races serves as an insult to antiblackness supremacy.

This account of racial evil distorts not just the contemporary racial context but also Porres'. In truth, ruling-class Peruvians imposed power over African-descended women and men not by pushing them away but by holding them too closely. Porres' racial climate therefore does resemble our own, but not in the way most of us think it does. Resembling their counterparts in Claver's Cartagena, the white inhabitants of seventeenth-century Lima strove to incorporate their city's sizable black population into their religion, culture, and society on their own terms. Black fugitivity threatened them much more than black proximity did; intimacy with Afro-Peruvians in fact could sometimes make Peruvian elites feel secure. Why? More than simply destroying the slave master's power, fugitivity can destroy the slave master himself. For this reason, white people feared the ever-expanding *palenques* that dotted the Peruvian countryside. Black Limeños could be fugitives even when they remained within city limits: "city officials accused [African-descended people] of being . . . violent

---

16. See for example, the 1937 article about Porres that ran in the Josephite—the missionary religious order dedicated to black ministry—magazine, *The Colored Harvest* as summarized in Cussen, *Black Saint of the Americas*, 194.

and ever on the lookout for ways to evade . . . their colonial masters."[17] For slaves, "far is free."[18]

As in Cartagena, Peruvian elites desired not distance from African-descended people, but the right type of proximity to them. Rather than seeking to expel black people from their midst, elite Peruvians strove to enlist them in their service, both materially and ideologically. Paradoxical perceptions of black people as exceptionally diseased and exceptionally skilled at healing exemplify antiblackness supremacy's dialectical relation to intimacy and distance. While the Spanish blamed freshly imported African-born slaves for triggering epidemics of measles, smallpox, yellow fever, and dysentery, they also credited Peruvians, especially mulattos, with special powers of healing as both surgeons and barbers and natural healers.[19] Peruvians of all backgrounds also considered healing as not simply a medical or natural phenomenon but also a deeply supernatural one. Therefore, just as African-descended people appeared especially able to heal and to infect, so they seemed uniquely in touch with the sacred as well as the demonic.[20] White people feared black people even as they relied upon them.

In many ways, the ambivalent role that Afro-Peruvians played in the city's cycles of sickness and health mirrored the ambivalent role they played in the life of the city itself: as slaves, their toil sustained the Spanish viceroyalty, but their fugitivity also threatened to destroy it. City elites therefore fought desperately to control Afro-Peruvians because they both needed and feared them. In this way, for example, just three months after Lima's founding, city officials "imposed on black slaves a curfew after dark, prohibited them from bearing arms, and stipulated punishments for those who left the city without permission."[21] Quite literally, Spanish whites could neither live with

---

17. Cussen, *Black Saint of the Americas*, 24.
18. As said by Marcellus to Kizzy in *Roots*, episode 3 (June 1, 2016), dir. Phillip Noyce, Mario Van Peebles, Thomas Carter, and Bruce Beresford.
19. Cussen, *Black Saint of the Americas*, 57, 81. The seventeenth-century barber shop offered its customers more than just a haircut or a shave. Barbers also pulled teeth and performed minor surgeries.
20. Ibid., 72–74.
21. Ibid., 24.

nor live without the blacks of Peru. Porres's status as barber and (super)natural healer must be understood in this context. Imbued with these skills, Porres enacted a comforting model of sanitized and sanitizing blackness. Rather than threatening either the antiblackness-supremacist social order or the white lives it sustained, Porres's extraordinary capacity for healing protected them. Porres used his blackness not to weaken the city and its elites but to strengthen them.[22]

6.2 Unkind Mercy: Porres as an Emblem of Racialized Slavery

This background helps us understand both why the witnesses who testified before his 1660 beatification proceedings submitted Porres's capacity to heal as the strongest evidence of his charitable character and why his "miraculous healing of Feliciano de Vega, a visiting bishop, was fundamental to the origins of Fray Martin's cult."[23] Exhibiting a remarkable aptitude for what Cussen terms "social healing," he also "reconciled friends, friars, and spouses." This capacity extended to the nonhuman animal realm: he also could bring animals of otherwise antagonistic species together.[24] Interpreted by Porres's first hagiographers as allegories for interracial relationships, these stories resonated particularly strongly with inhabitants of an unstable and sometimes chaotically interracial society such as colonial Peru.[25] But in bringing people together and in healing them, Porres does not disrupt racial hierarchy. In truth, it is not salutary to heal something that should be allowed to die, nor is it good to stitch together something that should be torn asunder.

These inter-species love stories reify white supremacy in another way. As an analogy for interracial relations, these anecdotes suggest that without pacifying intervention, interracial coexistence proves both difficult and dangerous. These stories also stress the distinction between wild animals, who endanger human life, and domesticated animals, who have been turned in to harmless pets. Certain animals

22. Ibid., 114.
23. Cussen, *Fray Martín de Porres*, 172.
24. Cussen, *Black Saint of the Americas*, 57.
25. Ibid., 89, 94.

are dangerous because they are wild: in stories about Porres, they repeatedly enter illicit spaces. Domesticated animals, on the other hand, are harmless largely because they remain inside the spatial boundaries Porres and other human keepers set for them. As a pious mulatto, Porres had managed to reconcile two violently opposed racial identities within his own body. So could he do the same for both humans and animals as well as the racial groups they symbolized.[26] Just as he tamed the black body that placed his own soul in mortal danger, so he did the same for the wild animals that menaced the monastery and the wild—indigenous and especially African—people who endangered the city and its elite inhabitants. Instructing formerly unruly mice as he counseled domesticated slaves at Limatambo, Porres exemplified the church's capacity to assist in projects of racial pacification.[27]

As with Claver's sainthood, Porres's sainthood embodies and sanctifies an ideology of racialized slavery precisely because it celebrates his kindness to racial "others." How? As portrayed by Porres's sainthood, nonhuman animals, which symbolize nonwhite Peruvians, can live as long as they stay in their place, that is, out of the monastery or in shackles.[28] Living not by right but by white largesse, nonhuman animals, like black people, need but can never earn white people's mercy. Porres's decision to let nonhuman animals live appears extraordinary only because they are believed to deserve to be put to death.[29] The symbolic resonance Porres' sainthood establishes between interspecies and interracial relationality proves not edifying but slavery-affirming.

Porres's mixed-race status only intensifies the racialized message conveyed by these allegories of animality. According to the thinking of his day, Porres's soul qualified as white not just because it successfully and often violently subordinated his black body but also because it housed the human being's higher faculties, namely, the reason and

26. Ibid., 199.
27. Kearns, *Life of Blessed Martin de Porres*, 111.
28. Cussen, *Black Saint of the Americas*, 119.
29. Kearns, *Life of Blessed Martin de Porres*, 111–12.

the will. Black people, by contrast, were identified with Porres's body because they shared not just its blackness but also its incapacity for self-rule. Lacking intelligence and self-discipline, black people appeared especially similar to non-human animals. In extending mercy to irrational animals, Porres also affirmed ideologies of black irrationality.[30]

Thus, while stories about Porres' interactions with non-human animals were originally intended to hide the interdependence between a master's mercy and his cruelty, when read in the context of slavery, they in fact illuminate it. In truth, a slave master can appear to act mercifully towards her slaves only because she is endowed with the power to punish them arbitrarily.[31] Consider an anecdote recounted in Cipriano de Medina's seventeenth century hagiography. According to him, one day, Porres healed a dog and then instructed him to refrain from urinating indoors in the future. Despite this warning, the dog "returned to his savage ways . . . [and] continued to misbehave until it was beaten by the friars and thrown out of the convent."[32] Porres offered kindness to non-human animals conditionally: if they refused to submit to his will, they could be subject to disciplining violence. Similarly, they were treated kindly only so that they would submit to his will. Therefore, just as Porres flagellated his own flesh because it was a "rebel slave," so he treated non-human animals tenderly only when and so that they would behave as obedient, that is, pacified slaves. Mercy upholds the power of a master over his slave just as surely as violence does.

Porres' sainthood sanctions racialized slavery in yet another way. Porres in fact appears merciful when he abstains from killing or physically disciplining disobedient non-human animals only if we believe that he is granting them something they do not inherently deserve. He similarly qualifies as kind only according to the logic of

---

30. Norbert Georges, "The Testimony of Father Fernando De Aragon," in Georges, *With Blessed Martin*, 158.
31. Norbert Georges, "Testimony of Catalina De Porres," in Georges, *With Blessed Martin*, 137–38; Georges, "Testimony of Father Fernando De Aragon," 156.
32. Cussen, *Fray Martín de Porres*, 173.

Africanized slavery, which figures the enslaved as a person who should have died—whether on the battlefield, on the gallows, or from starvation and poverty—except for the mercy of the master. In exchange for this merciful largesse, the master is owed unconditional obedience. Since the condemned person lives only because of the master, she must live for him alone. Lacking an independent right to life and self-determination, the ideology of slavery obliges enslaved people to live wherever and however their masters decree.

More than simply relating to nonhuman animals, Porres identified with them. In addition to frequently calling himself a "mulatto dog," Porres often insisted that his peers treat him like one.[33] For example, one time when he was extremely ill, a member of his congregation wanted to provide him comfort by putting sheets on his bed. Rather than accepting this gift, he rejected it, retorting, "For a mulatto dog, who would [ordinarily have] neither a thing to eat, nor a place to sleep, your illustrious Paternity orders him to lie down in sheets?"[34] Here Porres compares black people, including himself, to mangy dogs who would be foraging for scraps and shivering in the cold if not for the kindness of whites. As such, black people, like the non-human animals they resemble, ought to be grateful for whatever they receive, regardless of is adequacy.[35]

When we understand the crucial role that gratitude and kindness play in upholding a master's power, we are compelled to reconsider another aspect of Porres' hagiographical renown: his deigning to visit the slaves of Limatambo in order to instruct them in these lessons of racialized gratitude. Projecting contemporary notions of educational uplift upon him, contemporary hagiographers often have perceived this action as a type of affirmation of the humanity of the enslaved.[36] But while Porres certainly believed his enslaved students possessed a human soul, he taught them to not lift them up but hold them down. In this way, "when slaves working in the Dominican plantation at

33. Ibid., 91.
34. Cited in Garces, "Interspecies Logic of Race," 96–97.
35. Garces, "Interspecies Logic of Race," 99.
36. See, for example, Kearns, *Life of Blessed Martin de Porres*, 32–33, 43.

Limatambo complained about the lack of adequate food," Porres "would tell them that he, too, had not eaten because he did not yet deserve to eat." No wonder the city's Spanish and Creole elite believed him to be a good influence on both *bozales*—those newly arrived and purportedly undomesticated Africans—and purportedly "wild Indians" alike. In "entirely overlooking the differences between his fast and the regime of toil and hunger to which his pupils were subject," Porres deployed monastic ideals as an instrument of racial control.[37] In so doing, Porres expertly enlisted Catholic notions of piety in the service of slaveocracy, instructing enslaved black women and men that their salvation required that they submit to the slave master's lash.

Not all racially-conscious theologians would agree with my critique of Porres' sainthood. For example, contemporary theologian Alejandro García-Rivera argues that, rather than reifying racial hierarchy, these animal stories in particular and Porres' sainthood in general slyly subvert it. According to García-Rivera, in "crossing the boundary separating the animal domain from the man domain," Porres "challenges [an oppressive] . . . Ibero-European anthropology" and transforms it "into a new American anthropology."[38] When he convinced animals to eat together inter-specially, Porres created "a vision of cosmic and sacramental fellowship based on an anthropology of" not rational man over irrational beast but what he calls creatureliness. As revealed by these "eucharistic" feasts, "rationality [is not the] crucial rung defining humanity."[39] All creatures can eat together. For this reason, we become less human not when we either succumb to irrationality or submit to the powers of irrational creatures but when we "break . . . fellowship" with our fellow creatures both human and non-human.[40] For García-Rivera, sharing food across lines of difference serves as an antidote to and protest against the social evils of Porres' day: in "breaking the fellowship," he concludes that

37. Garces, "Interspecies Logic of Race," 97.
38. Alejandro García-Rivera, "St. Martin de Porres: Emblem of a Latin American Anthropology" (PhD diss., Lutheran School of Theology at Chicago, 1994), 92.
39. Ibid., 198.
40. Ibid., 217.

creatures "dim the imago dei and enslave the other."[41] As read by García-Rivera, Porres appears as a crusader for social justice and abolitionist.

But García-Rivera errs by assuming an overly general and therefore imprecise definition of racism. Antiblackness racism springs from the specific root of slavery. While slavery of course shares certain features with other forms of domination, it ultimately is distinct. Slave masters do not necessarily seek distance from their slaves; nor do they always keep them from their table. Like their counterparts in Cartagena, antiblackness-supremacist Limeños did not fear intimacy with black people as much as they feared losing control of them. They were threatened not by interracial intimacy or peaceful coexistence but by black fugitivity and disobedience. In promoting a social order in which wild blacks, like wild animals, have become tame and live alongside white people as pets, Porres does not subvert slavocracy; he helps to hold it together.

6.3 Porres and the Near Impossibility of White Humility

The racialized operation of Porres's sainthood proves even more apparent when contrasted to Claver's. Like Claver, the church recognizes Porres as a model of humility and selfless service. Yet Claver appears humble despite his willfully occupying a position of racial power and aggrandizement, while Porres qualifies as humble precisely because he accepts his status as less than white. Because Peruvian law barred people of African and indigenous descent from becoming full members of religious orders, Porres could enter Lima's Convent of the Most Holy Rosary only as a *donado*, a "lowest level assistant-server," for the Dominican friars in residence there. While his partial whiteness accorded him a status higher than the convent's black slaves, his half blackness made him the servant of whites: the order "initially refused to give him the habit" on account of his blackness.[42] Rather than

41. Ibid., 218.
42. Omar H. Ali, "The African Diaspora in Latin America: Afro-Peru and San Martín de Porres," *New African Review* 2, no. 4 (Summer 2013), http://tinyurl.com/h5lesrn, 3.

protesting this injustice, Porres embraced it. When Porres's superior sought to elevate his status a belated nine years later, some say as a result of the intervention of his white father, Porres resisted. Despite his lifelong service to the poor, Porres never received ordination as a priest. Porres's humility remained within the limits of blackness as defined by a white-supremacist society.

Prevalent notions of humility seemed to convince Porres that his racially subordinate status qualified as a blessing and a pathway to piety rather than an injustice. For example, while working as El Rosario's barber-surgeon, many of his white patients spat vicious racial slurs at him. Rather than turning the other cheek, Porres literally punched himself there: "When he disciplined himself late into the night, [he] could be heard repeating the same injurious words hurled at him during his rounds in the infirmary." Even more strikingly, when his priory was burdened with seemingly insurmountable debt, he reportedly told his superiors, "I am only a poor mulatto. Sell me. I am the property of the order. Sell me."[43] Claver, by contrast, committed himself to telling other women and men to be content with being sold.

Comparing the sainthoods of Claver and Porres further suggests that in addition to elevating racially specific standards of humility, the church tends to laud humility and debasement only when they are voluntary; in the Americas, black people suffered debasement involuntarily in a way that white people did not. White people appear saintly when they descend below the racially pristine status automatically accorded them, while people of color appear saintly only when they embrace the racial limits imposed upon them. But white people can never truly relinquish the prestige their bodies bring them while living within an antiblackness-supremacist society. As a result, the false humility of white people like Peter Claver seems heroic, while the often unrewarded struggle for human dignity of black Americans seems something less than saintly. For this reason, we ought to question whether white people inhabiting antiblackness-supremacist

43. John F. Fink, *American Saints: Five Centuries of Heroic Sanctity on the American Continents* (New York: Alba House, 2001), 11.

societies can ever display the humility of true saints. We ought to at least wonder whether white people can exercise such humility without seeking to dismantle regnant structures of antiblackness supremacy in both the church and society. Antiblackness supremacy cloaks white people in honor, and not even the most extreme display of evangelical charity can strip them of it.

Just as antiblackness supremacy makes white people seem more humble than they really are, so it makes blacks' struggles for justice, freedom, and dignity seem un-Christian, if not downright demonic. Would Porres have been recognized as a saint if he had protested the church's racially exclusionary practices? It seems unlikely. In counting Porres as its only black American saint, the church expresses implicit displeasure with those people whom James Cone describes as "'uppity' slaves, those who openly expressed their discontentment with servitude."[44] This uncritical Catholic celebration of humility also kept the church from "pronouncing God's judgment on human servitude and affirming that God created black people for freedom."[45] In reality, black people most invert the sinful order of a fallen world not when they descend into debasement but when they assert their self-worth, social equality, and status as beloved creatures of the God of justice. Operative Catholic ideologies of humility combine with pervasive antiblackness supremacy to diminish the church's collective capacity to recognize the black saints in its midst. In failing to understand the way notions of humility as debasement intersect with antiblackness supremacy, the church struggles to recognize black assertions of freedom and self-worth as saintly.[46]

---

44. James H. Cone, *God of the Oppressed*, 2nd ed. (Maryknoll, NY: Orbis, 1997), 193.
45. Ibid.
46. This helps explain why Catholic theology has failed to engage with figures like Malcolm X, despite the fact that "he speaks on behalf of those whom he calls the victims of America's 'so-called democracy'" (Bryan Massingale, "*Vox Victimarum Vox Dei*: Malcolm X as Neglected 'Classic' for Catholic Theological Reflection," *CTSA Proceedings* 65 [2010]: 63).

7

Catholic Sainthood and the Afterlife of Slavery

The church's memory of its racial saints has changed as the church and culture have evolved. More than mere historical figures, saints like Claver and Porres function as historically adaptable symbols of the church's self-image.[1] The subjective adaptability of the church's hagiographical memory is not in and of itself bad.[2] But in the case of Claver and Porres, this plasticity has allowed contemporary Catholics to imagine these saints as symbols not of what the church was but of what they wish it had been. Despite the antiracist aspirations of many of their champions, the saintly afterlives of both of these South Americans in fact embody and perpetuate antiblackness supremacy in three primary ways: first, they promote a servile ideology of black gratitude for implicitly white ecclesial saviors; second, they misrepresent the character of racial evil in both the past and the present; and third, they deflect the extent of the church's corporately

1. Michel de Certeau, *The Writing of History* (New York: Columbia University Press, 1988), 272, 280.
2. Certainly, none of the aforementioned Catholics would deny that Claver was flawed, but they believe Claver's ministry to the blacks truly saintly.

vicious participation in antiblackness supremacy. These sainthoods therefore also have limited the church's capacity to embody corporate racial virtue in the present.

Because Catholics typically have misunderstood slavery, so they have misidentified its afterlife. Just as racialized slavery appears less evil than it actually was when we define it too broadly, so does slavery's ongoing afterlife. In the afterlife of slavery, antiblackness supremacy attempts to uphold the stigmatizing association between blackness and slave status. Moreover, insofar as the afterlife of slavery structures the world, so it pervades the church—and the church enacts this evil in distinctly Catholic fashion. In particular, the ecclesial afterlife of slavery manifests itself primarily in a perverse attachment to black gratitude; an immoderate fear of black rebellion; an uncritical celebration of interracial proximity, affection, and love; an insatiable desire for white saviors and heroes; and a misplaced desire to elevate white heroes. In order to make this argument, this chapter first provides a brief overview of the history of each saint's afterlife and then offers a critique. It aims to enhance the church's capacity to build racial virtue by sharpening its ability to recognize its racial vices.

7.1 Corporate Vindication: Claver and Catholic Racial Triumphalism

Although Claver was beatified relatively quickly, Vatican officials initially declined to canonize him because of the way he physically abused black slaves. Partially for this reason, his cause languished for nearly a century.[3] But in 1747, Pope Benedict XIV repaired Claver's reputation when he argued thus:

> If we take into careful consideration the obstinate disposition of the Moors, and the savageness of their nature; the contempt exhibited towards his previous warnings [against their improper dances]; his great suavity of manners . . . [in addition to] all those acts of beautiful charity and benevolence towards the Africans, who looked upon him as their father and benefactor . . . [and] the well-known facts that from such blows

---

3. Germeten, "Century of Promoting Saint Peter Claver," 25.

no asperity of feeling was ever engendered against him . . . no cause for condemnation will be found.[4]

Pope Benedict XIV accepts the logic of slave mastership: Claver beat black slaves because he had to, and they did not mind it anyway. This declaration cleared the way for Pope Pius IX to "approve and accept the several miracles Claver was said to have performed in his lifetime" a little more than a century later, in 1848.[5]

The cause of Claver's sainthood would gain momentum thereafter. In 1868, shortly after the United States ratified the Thirteenth Amendment, the Jesuit priest Joseph Finotti began to promote Claver's story for the way it provided "a pattern to those who earnestly and honestly work for the elevation of a down-trodden race" and who "will not allow that a difference in color should be a line of demarcation between souls." According to Finotti, Claver models "Christian patience and brotherly love," which he identifies as the "only. . . path that will lead to a sure [racial] triumph."[6] To this end, Claver purportedly "did for the slaves . . . all the good that they were susceptible of, for the time being."[7] To African-Americans, Finotti portrayed Claver as an example "of a paternalistic European to whom they should be thankful."[8] Rather than saving themselves, black people ought to be grateful that they have been saved by whites. Habituated by Africanized slavery and its incipient afterlife, Finotti considers black gratitude to white priestly heroes as a means to racial peace. He urges white people to love black people, but he does not seem to believe they owe black people justice.

A few decades later, Catholic leaders in the United States and Europe began to popularize Claver in order to promote what I term a Catholic racial triumphalism vis-á-vis both Protestantism and Islam.[9] The most

---

4. Quoted in Joseph M. Finotti, *Peter Claver: A Sketch of His Life and Labors in Behalf of the African Slave* (Boston: Lee & Shephard, 1868), 69.
5. Germeten, "Century of Promoting Saint Peter Claver," 26.
6. Ibid., 28.
7. Finotti, *Peter Claver*, 15–17, as cited in ibid.
8. Ibid.
9. For example, see Slattery, *Life of St. Peter Claver*, 10; Brioschi, *Vida de san Pedro Claver*, 83; Pope Leo XIII, *In Plurimis: Encyclical of Pope Leo XIII on the Abolition of Slavery*, no. 20 (1888), http://tinyurl.com/zapmb5c.

significant articulation of the anti-Islamic component of this Claverian Catholic racial triumphalism appears in Pope Leo's June 1888 encyclical, *In Plurimis*. The year 1888 was a geopolitically pivotal one: just as the abolition of slavery in Brazil had finally ended black slavery in the Americas, the European imperial scramble for Africa was just beginning. Un-coincidentally canonized in the first month of 1888, Claver was the perfect saint for this year: in addition to evidencing the church's tireless opposition to slavery, Claver's sainthood could also be used to sanction the evangelizing mission that would accompany and solidify Europe's late nineteenth-century colonization of Africa.[10] Claver's sainthood could in fact present the purported fact of the former as an argument for the moral goodness of latter: European Christians ought to rule black people in Africa because of how well they had ruled them in the Americas. Thus, more than simply commemorating the abolition of black slavery in Brazil, *In Plurimis* also presented a theological argument for colonizing Africa.

To these ends, Leo argued that the church had always "protected slaves . . . from the savage anger and cruel injuries of their masters."[11] According to Pope Leo, the Catholic church ultimately has acted as a tireless abolitionist, "cutting out and destroying this dreadful curse of slavery . . . tenderly and with [great] prudence." Evidencing this, Pope Leo claims that the church denounced and opposed the African slave trade from the moment of its mid-fifteenth-century inception.[12] Pope Leo also identifies the church as an instrument of freedom for the way in which it purportedly has liberated human beings of all races from the most damning form of bondage: enslavement to sin.[13]

Pope Leo does not deny that Catholics owned slaves, whether corporately or as individuals. He instead presents a sanitized history of Christian mastership in which the slavery established by the church

10. "One of the chief justifications for this so-called 'Scramble for Africa' was a desire to stamp out slavery" (Saul David, " Slavery and the 'Scramble for Africa,'" BBC History, February 17, 2011, http://tinyurl.com/9hpg2oc); W. E. B. Dubois, *Black Folk Then and Now: An Essay in the History and Sociology of the Negro Race* (New York: Oxford University Press, 2007), 164.
11. Leo XIII, *In Plurimis*, paras. 10, 12–14.
12. Ibid., paras. 15–16.
13. Ibid., para. 6.

fathers differed from its pagan predecessors for the way it uniquely recognized that "the rights of masters extended lawfully indeed over the works of their slaves, but that their power did not extend to using horrible cruelties against their persons."[14] Articulating an argument that white Catholics in the United States would use against their Protestant counterparts, Pope Leo assures the reader that, unlike the Greeks and Romans before them, these early Christians held slaves not with "cruelty and wickedness" but "great gentleness and humanity."[15]

Just as Pope Leo claims that Christians helped to protect slaves by holding them captive, so he argues that the church has opposed slavery precisely by making sure it did not end too soon. For Pope Leo, the church has promoted emancipation by resisting abolitionism. Rather than pursuing what he deems "precipitate action in securing the manumission and liberation of the slaves," the church instead has ensured "that the minds of the slaves should be instructed through her discipline in the Christian faith, and with baptism should acquire habits suitable to the Christian." To merely emancipate enslaved people without reforming them, he insists, "would have entailed tumults and wrought injury, as well to the slaves themselves as to the commonwealth."[16] The racially violent theory of freedom that elevated Claver to saintly fame still prevailed more than two hundred years after his beatification: like Claver's early advocates, Pope Leo believed that the church best liberates enslaved people by ensuring they are enslaved by Christian masters.

Like Claver and his first hagiographers, Pope Leo also identified slave rebellion against Christian masters as not just immoral but unlikely. Strangely overlooking the successful revolution that occurred in French-owned Haiti just a century prior, Pope Leo celebrates the fact that "history has no case to show of Christian slaves for any other cause setting themselves in opposition to their masters of joining in conspiracies against the State." The church has had a morally salutary effect on enslaved people, convincing them to resist not their bondage,

14. Ibid., para. 10.
15. Ibid., para. 9.
16. Ibid.

which is lawful, but only "the wicked commands of those above them to the holy law of God." In helping enslaved people to obey their Christian masters happily, the church has promoted the "fraternal unanimity which should exist between Christians."[17]

Largely because the Catholic church alone could liberate those black people who had been transported out of Africa, so it retains this power with respect to those women and men who remain there. Just as the Africans who were held as slaves in the Americas had been liberated from enslavement to sin, so modern-day Africans awaited liberation from "Mohammadeans [who deem] Ethiopians and men of similar nations ... very little superior to brute beasts" and therefore steal them away into a "barbarous" slave trade that transpired not by sea but over land.[18] For Pope Leo, as for Claver, the Middle Passage represented not a trail of terror but a path to true freedom and salvation because it brought purportedly pagan Africans under the power of white Christians. Because the trans-Saharan slave trade, on the other hand, brings black-skinned people under the sway of Muslims, it qualifies as cruel and dehumanizing.

Because it helps "apostolic men ... find out how best they can secure the safety and liberty of slaves," Pope Leo praises the "new roads [that] are being made and [the] new commercial enterprises [that are being] undertaken in the lands of Africa."[19] According to Pope Leo, even those Europeans who seek merely financial gain in Africa do God's work. Any action that weakens Muslim sovereignty serves God's glory. For Pope Leo, the Berlin Conference therefore inaugurated an era not of plunder but of liberation.[20] Like Claver's first champions, Pope Leo located black liberation in not freedom but subordination to European Christians.

Claver's sainthood helped Pope Leo pursue both of these ends. In addition to coordinating Claver's canonization with the abolition of

17. Ibid., para. 10.
18. Ibid., para. 18.
19. Ibid., para. 20.
20. For more on Pope Leo XIII's collaboration with Belgian's King Leopold to send Catholic missionaries to the Congo, see Charles de T'Serclaes de Wommersom, *The Life and Labors of Pope Leo XIII: With a Summary of His Important Letters, Addresses, and Encyclicals* (Chicago: Rand, McNally, 1903), 206; Justin McCarthy, *Pope Leo XIII*, Public Men of To-Day (New York: Frederick Warne, 1896), 148–49.

slavery in Brazil, Pope Leo also proposed Peter Claver as a model of "apostolic virtue" whom contemporary European colonizers of Africa ought to emulate: according to Pope Leo, white Catholics ought to

> look at [Claver] who for forty years gave himself up to minister with the greatest constancy in his labors, to a most miserable assembly of Moorish slaves. . . . If they endeavor to take to themselves and reflect the charity and patience of such a man, they will shine indeed as worthy ministers of salvation, authors of consolation, messengers of peace, who, by God's help, may turn solicitude, desolation, and fierceness into the most joyful fertility of religion and civilization.[21]

In order to sharpen the contrast between liberating Catholicism and tyrannical Islam, Pope Leo reverts back to older ways of naming Africanized slaves. Although this way of speaking had fallen mostly out of fashion, he identifies contemporary Africans as "Moorish." Just as the Iberian peninsula had to be reconquered by Christian sovereigns, so do the bodies and souls of contemporary black Africans. Pope Leo canonizes Claver largely due to the way he appears to lead African people out of the enslaving barbarism of Islam into the civilizing liberation of Christianity. In Leo's view as in Claver's, Africans ought not liberate themselves; they receive liberation at the hands of white masters.

7.2 Claver and White Fantasies of Black Gratitude

Catholic racial triumphalism served a different purpose in the United States. Rather than helping Catholics to defeat Europe's Muslim imperial rivals, it attempted to lure black people away from Protestant denominations. In pursuit of this aim, Catholic clerics argued that Catholic masters in South America purportedly treated their chattel much more humanely than did their Dutch and English Protestant counterparts because the Catholic church alone recognized that black slaves were spiritually equal to their masters. Presenting this history as evidence that the contemporary Catholic church would protect and

---

21. Leo XIII, *In Plurimis*, para. 20.

defend the human dignity of the so-called Negro better than the Protestants could, some Catholic apologists deployed it as a strategy by which to evangelize blacks.[22] This argument also enabled a growing immigrant church to claim its place in a resolutely Protestant nation. By proving that the Catholic church was good for black people, Claver's sainthood supposedly proved that it was good for the country as well.

But why did they deem the church good in these ways? Catholic racial apologists proposed Claver as racial antidote because they believed he would civilize and pacify blacks. More than simply underestimating the cruelty of even Catholic slave mastership, these apologists also made excuses for contemporary ideologies of white mastership. Above all, late-nineteenth- and early-twentieth-century Jesuit champions of Claver, such as John Slattery and William Markoe, upheld slavery's afterlife precisely by expecting black people to express gratitude for not just Claver but also themselves and their church. Claver's story inspired the white Jesuit priest John Slattery to found the Josephite Fathers, a priestly order dedicated to ministering exclusively to black Catholics, in 1871. Today, he is lauded as "the preeminent Catholic evangelist to the freedmen."[23] Unfortunately, despite his sincere commitment to racial justice, neither Slattery's hagiographical imagination nor his politics could overcome his vicious racial habituation. In particular, Slattery possessed a romantic attachment to his own white saviorship and that of his putatively white Catholic Church. To this end, he strenuously insisted that "only the church had the means to elevate the Negro race morally and spiritually."[24] For this reason, Slattery also believed the Catholic Church possessed a unique capacity to save the nation itself. In training formerly enslaved black women and men, Slattery declared that his church would thereby protect the United States from "impending

22. Some of these hagiographers sincerely disdained what they perceived as racial injustice. One author, Fr. John Richard Slattery, even recognized the link between slavery and present-day inequalities, arguing, "In place of the slave-ship, we have built the cheap, badly built tenements; instead of the middle passage, there are now the back streets and alleys" (*Life of St. Peter Claver*, 11).
23. William L. Portier, "John R. Slattery's Vision for the Evangelization of American Blacks," *U.S. Catholic Historian* 5, no. 1 (1986): 20.
24. Ibid., 26.

racial conflict" that many feared would occur "as the Blacks grew in population and education." Just as the church "changed the Hun, the Goth, and the Vandal into the nations which today make up Europe," so he promised that it could transform blacks into civilized and well-behaved citizens.[25]

Because he blamed black people's incivility and violent irrationality on the environmental damage done by slavery, Slattery might appear to be a step ahead of those whites who attributed black people's inferiority to some biologically permanent essence. Unlike these biological racists, his cultural racism led him to believe that black people could be improved with proper training, at least in theory. But we should not overstate the differences between these two forms of racism. Slattery nonetheless held that black people were inherently incapable of self-rule; he perceived civilization as a gift that only white authority figures could give blacks. He maintained that although "the slave may be emancipated, the freedman must be developed." Making this ideology even more explicit, he professed that "neither by nature nor by traditional training can the colored people, taken as a body, stand as yet on the same footing of moral independence as their white brethren."[26] As if intentionally parroting Claver's racial philosophy, Slattery claimed that black people could acquire equality with whites only by being treated differently from them, just as they could attain independence from whites only if they were first deprived of it. Rather than deviating from them, Slattery's paternalism therefore actually revived older ideologies of racialized slavery.

Further clarifying Slattery's alliance with slavery's afterlife, Slattery's desire to play savior to black people only intensified his commitment to pacifying them. A memory shared by one of Slattery's biographers highlights the affective connection between white saviorship and black pacification. Although Slattery "continually protested [both] the racist admissions policies" at Catholic colleges and universities as well as the blockade against black priests, he

25. Ibid.
26. Ibid., 36.

"considered the same protests coming from Blacks as tactically unwise . . . counseling passivity and submission."[27] Like the nomadic and unsettled barbarian tribes that would not allow themselves to be enfolded into the Roman imperium, the freedwomen and -men posed a "mortal threat" to the United States and its white citizens as long as they remained outside of white control.[28] Like Claver's previous admirers, Slattery both perceives black fugitivity as essentially violent and perceives Catholic evangelization as a way to stem "apocalyptic predictions of impending racial conflict."[29]

Even relative antiracists like Slattery still believed that black people lacked the capacity for self-rule, even after slavery's abolition. This affective holdover from the antebellum era unleashed a tension in Slattery's psyche: his commitment to black freedom and equality consistently clashed with and was sometimes trumped by his desire to be adored by black people almost as though he were their master. He wanted black people to love his church in this way as well. We should not, therefore, be surprised that Slattery perceived Claver as a kindred spirit. Precisely because "the atmosphere surrounding the Negro missions [today] is about the same as Claver found it in Cartagena," Slattery believed that Claver's ability to overcome these circumstances would "inspire our American youth with a thirst for the salvation of the millions of their Black Countrymen."[30] Claver's life story also reassured young white men that the gratitude of the black masses would be their steady reward. Repeatedly, Slattery mentioned the extreme gratitude that the black slaves of Cartagena lavished upon Claver: ultimately, he promised, "the poor slaves knew not how to express their gratitude" to him.[31]

White expectations of black gratitude would continue to shape the way white priests related to black people well into the twentieth century. In his 1920 hagiography, white Jesuit priest William Markoe

27. Ibid., 34.
28. Portier, "John R. Slattery's Vision," 26.
29. Ibid., 26.
30. Slattery, *Life of St. Peter Claver*, 11.
31. William Morgan Markoe, *The Slave of the Negroes* (Chicago: Loyola University Press, 1920), 61.

explained that black people are never more grateful "than when a generous champion has come forward to defend their too oft violated rights."[32] Lamentably, however, despite the fact that Claver was the greatest champion of the black race in history, he remained "unknown to the vast majority of American Negroes." If they knew Claver, Markoe was sure that black people "would never suffer him, who did so much for their race, to remain in obscurity, unthanked and unloved." Putting his faith into action, Markoe wrote his hagiography of Claver "in the hopes that this hero may be better known to the Colored people of America."[33]

But Markoe did not write for the sake of Claver's reputation alone. He believed that as black people's gratitude to white saviors such as Claver increased, so would their gratitude for and attachment to the Catholic church. In so doing, Claver would also help black people adhere to their given nature; according to Markoe, "the colored race possesses three special virtues, namely, gratitude, affection, and a deep-rooted spirit of religion." Like all virtues, these are connected: in "arousing within [black people] sincere sentiments of gratitude and affection" for the church, they may receive "a deeper and truer spirit of religion than even that which they are known to possess."[34] Markoe defines blackness and black religiosity as inherently oriented towards and fulfilled by expressions of gratitude towards white ecclesial saviors.

Not just on paper, but also in life Markoe strove to make black people more grateful to Catholic men such as him. In this way, Markoe allied with another pro-Claver white Jesuit named John La Farge in order to expel the gifted lay black Catholic activist Thomas Wyatt Turner as president of the Federated Colored Catholics (FCC), even though Turner had founded this organization and directed it skillfully.[35] La Farge justified this coup by explaining that "the colored man's

32. Ibid.
33. Ibid.
34. Ibid., 3, 61. For another example of this hagiographical trope, see Georges, *With Blessed Martin de Porres*, 41–42.
35. David W. Southern, *John La Farge and the Limits of Catholic Interracialism, 1911-1963* (Baton Rouge: Louisiana State University Press, 1996), 140–45.

destinies are safest and surest when in the hands of [at that time almost exclusively white] Catholic leaders and Catholic educators." La Farge then proclaimed himself the head of the FCC and rechristened it the Catholic Interracial Council. Its magazine, *The Interracial Review*, unsurprisingly featured more stories about Peter Claver than any other saint, with Martín de Porres and then Pierre Toussaint following not too far behind him.

Markoe ousted Turner for theological reasons. According to Markoe, in desiring that the FCC remain primarily for and by black Catholics, Turner proved that he had "a little of Black Muslim in him" and was therefore unfit for leadership.[36] As if harking back to the origins of antiblackness supremacy, when fifteenth-century Iberian Christians began to justify the enslavement of Africans on the grounds that they qualified as black Moors, Markoe unwittingly revealed the tenacity and longevity of racial habits.[37] Slurring Turner as a "black Muslim" because he rebelled against white authority, Markoe linked authentic blackness to not just Christian status but also the racialized docility he believed it ought to secure. Like many white people do even today, here Markoe seemingly embodied a history of which he may have been completely unaware.

In comparison to the vast majority of their white Catholic contemporaries, people such as Slattery and Markoe admittedly were among the most racially progressive white Catholics of their time. Yet, rather than vindicating them, these good intentions only underscore the racial limitations of regnant Catholic notions of holiness. Much like Claver himself, these white Catholics could not promote the welfare of their black countrywomen and men without also advancing slavery's ecclesial afterlife.

The role that Claver's sainthood has played in promoting ideologies

36. Raymond A. Schroth, *The American Jesuits: A History* (New York: New York University Press, 2007), 121.
37. Kenneth Wolf, "The 'Moors' of West Africa and the Beginnings of the Portuguese Slave Trade," *Pomona Faculty Publications and Research*, January 1, 1994, 451, 454; Jonathan Schorsch, *Jews and Blacks in the Early Modern World* (Cambridge: Cambridge University Press, 2004), 147; Debra Blumenthal, *Enemies and Familiars: Slavery and Mastery in Fifteenth-Century Valencia* (Ithaca, NY: Cornell University Press, 2009), 22, 42–44.

of black gratitude cannot be blamed on these three individuals alone. For example, in paintings and statues, Claver is almost always portrayed in the company of one or more discernibly black males who are nearly always physically smaller than him.[38] Often the black people who appear alongside Claver are not just infantilized men but also actual children and babies. Claver typically is placed in a position of paternal protection over these black men. These visual pieces of hagiography function in today's world much like Claver did in his own. More than simply enforcing white people's dominance over their black subordinates, these works simultaneously assure white people that, like children, black people can never truly revolt. Perhaps even more important, they signal that, like well-behaved children, blacks do not want to revolt.

7.3 The Knights and Ladies of Peter Claver

Admittedly, the existence of the Knights and Ladies of Saint Peter Claver, the oldest black Catholic fraternal and sororal organization in the United States, may seem to discredit my critique of Claver entirely. Indeed, if black Catholics decided to name themselves after him, how can his sainthood function in the way that I claim it does? Ought we not trust the historical judgments of generations of black Catholics over the opinion of a single white theologian? Yes, we should accord a certain epistemological privilege to the Knights and Ladies of Peter Claver; however, black Catholics' selecting him as a namesake does not qualify as an exoneration of either his sainthood or the church's memory of him. Thus, although I write this book in order to critique the way that white people and, to a lesser extent, other nonblack people have used the sainthood of Claver to advance their racial

38. See, for example, the picture of Claver used in a story about him on Catholic Online, accessed June 6, 2016, http://tinyurl.com/llrvh2; the picture used on the website for the Catholic television channel EWTN, September 4, 2011, http://tinyurl.com/j2x3gr4; the one used by *Legatus* magazine, September 1, 2009, http://tinyurl.com/zdfrah3; the one used in *Dominicana* magazine, a publication of Saint Joseph Province of the Order of Preachers, September 9, 2015, http://tinyurl.com/jsv3b65; the image on the website of Irish monks living at Silverstream Priory under the Rule of Saint Benedict, September 9, 2006, http://tinyurl.com/jut33jw; the Claver Foundation prayer card, accessed June 6, 2016, http://tinyurl.com/jaf4yz4; and the image used by the Catholic News Agency, November 15, 2009, http://tinyurl.com/j78f8ex.

agendas and have no desire, and even less of a right, to tell black Catholics how to relate to the church's past or to live within its imperfect structures, I still must place my project in conversation with the Knights and Ladies of Saint Peter Claver.

The existence of a black sodality named after Claver does not authorize non-black Catholics to celebrate him. One, in seeking a saint to model their lives after, Catholics of African descent living in the Americas had few choices. When black Catholics sought to select a "patron saint who would have a divine interest in the progress of this Organization for the advancement of the African American people," whom else could they have selected? At the time of the Knights of Peter Claver's 1909 founding, the church had yet to canonize even a single American saint of African descent. Martín de Porres would not receive canonization until the late date of 1962. Peter Claver truly was the best the church had to offer African Americans. This fact should disturb us.

Second, while Claver's sainthood endorses an ideology of white mastership, African-American Catholics who joined the Knights of Peter Claver did not capitulate to the church's regnant white supremacy; they instead sought to "make a way out of no way."[39] Just by claiming their place in a church that often did not want them, those who belonged to the Knights and Ladies of Peter Claver paradoxically subverted the racial order that Claver condoned.[40] These black

---

39. Monica A. Coleman, *Making a Way Out of No Way: A Womanist Theology* (Minneapolis: Fortress Press, 2008). As Coleman explains, "'Making a way out of no way' means that the way forward was not contained in the past alone, the only way that was known. A way forward, a way toward life, comes from another source. It comes from unforeseen possibilities. These possibilities come from God" (34). Coleman relates this phrase to womanist theology: "'Making a way out of no way' is a central theme in black women's struggles and God's assistance in helping them to overcome oppression. [It] can serve as a summarizing concept for the ways that various womanist theologians describe God's liberation of black women" (9).

40. LaReine-Marie Mosely, "Daniel A. Rudd and His *American Catholic Tribune*: Faithful and Prophetic in Passing On the Tradition," in *Uncommon Faithfulness: The Black Catholic Experience*, ed. M. Shawn Copeland (Maryknoll, NY: Orbis, 2009); Albert J. Raboteau, "Relating Race and Religion: Four Historical Models," in Copeland, *Uncommon Faithfulness*, 1–6; Cyprian Davis, "The Holy See and American Black Catholics: A Forgotten Chapter in the History of the American Church," *U.S. Catholic Historian* 7, nos. 2–3 (1988): 157–81; Lincoln R. Rice, "Confronting the Heresy of 'The Mythical Body of Christ': The Life of Dr. Arthur Falls," *American Catholic Studies* 123, no. 2 (2012): 59–77; John T. McGreevy, *Parish Boundaries: The Catholic Encounter with Race in the Twentieth-Century Urban North* (Chicago: University Of Chicago Press, 1998); Karen J. Johnson, "The Universal Church in the Segregated City: Doing Catholic Interracialism in Chicago, 1915–1963" (PhD diss., The University of Illinois at Chicago, 2013).

Catholics' commitment to the Catholic Church does not validate the integrationist aspirations of Claverites like Slattery and Markoe. While these white priests used Claver in order to encourage other white Catholics to reach out to black Catholics and pull them in, the Knights and Ladies of Peter Claver deployed his memory in order either to push their way in or to refuse to be pushed out.

In practice, of course, the evangelizing efforts of white priests and religious, such as Slattery, Markoe, and La Farge, were not entirely disconnected from the experience of black Catholics. Still, in the afterlife of black slavery, the active, ecclesial self-determination pursued by the Knights and Ladies of Peter Claver possesses a different racial meaning than corresponding attempts by white Catholic clerics to make black Catholics the passive object of white salvation. Nobody operates with entirely unrestrained free agency. But in the former case, black Catholics attempted to move themselves, even as they strategically collaborated with certain white Catholics. In the latter case, white Catholic clerics attempted to create a situation in which black people would be moved by whites.

Unsurprisingly, then, while white Claverites often perpetuated Claver's racial ideology, the Knights and Ladies of Peter Claver corporately undermined it. In seeking to build a brotherhood that "would assure [African Americans] a measure of financial strength in times of sickness and death," the founders already disobeyed Claver's desire that black people remain unnaturally dependent on white masters for survival and salvation.[41] Further discrediting Claver's belief that black people ought to be catechized like dim-witted children through pictures and signs, the Knights of Peter Claver hosted "study clubs and discussion groups on the church and its doctrines as well as topics concerning the common welfare of men and nations."[42] While Claver insisted that black Catholics remain always under white supervision, the Knights of Peter Claver possessed an all-black leadership team, elected by them and for them. Unlike Claver, who

41. Abston, "Catholicism and African-Americans," 94.
42. Ibid., 99.

wanted even black adults to remain his children forever, in 1939 the Knights of Peter Claver began to demand that black Catholic men also be allowed to be priests.[43]

Further differentiating the Knights of Peter Claver from their patron saint, since 1953 the Knights have pursued an explicit, corporate commitment to racial equality.[44] In addition to helping organizations like the NAACP agitate for equal pay among black and white teachers in New Orleans, the Knights and Ladies also helped to expand the Voting Rights Act of 1965. While Peter Claver strove to save black souls by enslaving their bodies, the Knights and Ladies of Peter Claver have sought the liberation of the entire human person. The Knights and Ladies of Peter Claver also place themselves in imitation not of Claver but of his enslaved so-called assistants, who often did not assist Claver as much as they ministered in his place. While white advocates of Claver continue to overlook the personhood of his slaves in this way, the Knights and Ladies help to restore it. More than simply resurrecting their memory, the Knights and Ladies affirm these enslaved persons as models of holiness that surpass that offered by their captor.[45]

More than simply calling attention to the fact that "the slave of the slaves" was actually their master, identifying with Claver's slaves simultaneously can work against Claver's ecclesiology of white power. While Claver insisted that black women and men could enter the church only as slaves, these black Catholics position themselves within the church as knights and ladies. In so doing, they claim for themselves the honor and dignity that Claver would have denied them. Since they also retroactively label Claver's slaves as "the real first Knights and Ladies of Peter Claver," they also remind the church of the rights these men deserved but were denied.[46] They further demonstrate that these

43. Theda Skocpol and Jennifer Lynn Oser, "Organization despite Adversity: The Origins and Development of African American Fraternal Organizations," *Social Science History* 28 (2004): 391.
44. Abston, "Catholicism and African-Americans," 212–13.
45. "History of the Knights of Peter Claver, Inc." http://nbccongress.org/spotlight/history-knights-of-peter-claver.asp. Accessed June 21, 2016.
46. "History of the Knights of Peter Claver, Inc." http://nbccongress.org/spotlight/history-knights-of-peter-claver.asp. Accessed June 21, 2016.

men were enslaved not despite Claver's otherwise admirable piety and religious devotion but precisely because of it. As the example of the Knights and Ladies of Peter Claver suggests, perhaps the church best remembers Claver by remembering his slaves.

In remembering Claver's sainthood in this way, we also better position ourselves to construct a theology of black slavery. Rather than pointing to God's presence, Claver's sainthood in fact reveals where God was absent. Claver's canonization also reminds the church that, at least in the case of black slavery, the church failed to corporately discern the difference. The god of Peter Claver—the one who orchestrated the enslavement of African women, children, and men—is not the God who liberated the Israelites or whose son vowed to "set the captives free."[47] A church that perceives Peter Claver as an icon of Christ cannot act as an agent of black life and liberation.

Non-black Catholics, especially when white, cannot turn Claver into an icon of racial goodness, no matter how hard we try.[48] Even explicitly anti-racist reconfigurations of Claver's memory inevitably endorse an ideology of white saviorhood. Contemporary Catholics overestimate Claver's racial benevolence in large part because they misunderstand the relation between slavery and intimacy. Indeed, Claver participated in anti-blackness supremacy not by pushing black people away but by holding them close. When white Catholics name their ministries and communities after Claver, they style themselves in his image, especially when their work aims at predominately or disproportionately black populations.

If we ought not to rehabilitate Claver, then we might wish to seek distance from him, relegating him to a deliberately forgotten past. But this strategy would serve as just another way of denying the church's historical alliance with white supremacy. We instead should accord

---

47. Gustavo Gutiérrez, *A Theology of Liberation: History, Politics, and Salvation*, trans. Caridad Inda and John Eagleson, rev. ed. (Maryknoll, NY: Orbis, 1988), 69, 86.

48. Von Germeten notes that Ann Roos's 1965 work of young adult fiction, *Peter Claver: Saint among Slaves*, "is perhaps the first book on Claver that presents the saint in a way that would appeal to a twenty-first century reader" ("Century of Promoting Claver," 36). More recently, see for example, James Martin, *The Jesuit Guide to (Almost) Everything: A Spirituality for Real Life* (New York: Harper Collins, 2010), 245–46; and Brandon Vogt, *Saints Guide to Social Justice* (Huntington, IN: Our Sunday Visitor, 2014), 35–36.

Claver and his sainthood a more prominent place in the church's collective imagination—not to celebrate him, but so that we can recognize ourselves more clearly. Claver's sainthood ought to serve as a vehicle for corporate repentance. As Cardinal Edward Cassidy affirmed, all those who belong to the body of Christ "are linked to the sins as well as the merits of all [the church's] children."[49]

7.4 The Limits of Memory: Porres and the Struggle for Black Civil Rights

Ought we judge the historiography of Martín de Porres's hagiography as critically? Unfortunately, the story of how Porres came to be known as the patron saint of mixed-black and mixed-race people also has unfolded within the confines of antiblackness supremacy. Porres' saintly afterlife holds much in common with Claver's. First, both saints are considered defenders of ideals and entities that would not have existed as such during their earthly lifetimes: African Americans, the Republic of Colombia, and human rights in the case of Claver, and African Americans and racial harmony in the case of Porres.

Second, just as the majority of Claver's hagiographers in the late-nineteenth and early-twentieth centuries were Jesuits, many of Porres's hagiographers belonged to the Dominican order. The Dominicans, more than any other group, helped to turn Porres into a racial icon of the twentieth century. Third, Porres's champions also have tended to be the most racially righteous members of the Catholic Church. As with those who promoted Claver's memory, their best efforts proved no match for their bad racial habits. Rather than uncritically condemning these reformers, this survey uncovers the way in which the vice of antiblackness supremacy inhabited the minds even of those white Catholics who attempted to do right by black folks. Fourth, early twentieth century hagiographers repeatedly cited Porres'

49. Presentation by Cardinal Edward Idris Cassidy before the Commission for Religious Relations with the Jews, "We Remember: A Reflection on the Shoah," March 16, 1998. http://www.vatican.va/roman_curia/pontifical_councils/chrstuni/documents/rc_pc_chrstuni_doc_16031998_shoah_en.html.

mixed race status to establish the Catholic church as the champion of "the Negro race." For example, the white Dominican priest J. C. Kearns describes his ministry and nineteenth century beatification as "clear indications of the spiritual democracy of the church" while the Blessed Martin de Porres Guild—a white Catholic organization founded to promote his canonization—points to these facts to evidence "the equality of the moral obligation and the aristocracy of virtue in the Church."[50]

Consider the 1937 hagiography written by the aforementioned Dominican priest J. C. Kearns. Despite Kearns's relatively advanced racial politics, he still endorsed many aspects of the proslavery ideology that had animated earlier hagiographies. And although Kearns wrote more than seventy years after the abolition of slavery, Kearns particularly admired Porres's purported ability to pacify the black slaves who worked at Limatambo. According to Kearns, when these brutalized laborers expressed what he considered unholy "bitterness and a desire for revenge" against their masters, Porres would "tactfully and with a deep understanding of human nature, explain the folly of such sentiments."[51] Yet Kearns somehow still described Porres as "striving to set aside the barriers of racial prejudice and injustice . . . with all the ardor of his soul."[52] In so doing, Kearns attributed to Porres a belief in and a commitment to racial equality that Porres simply did not possess.

Kearns only appears to contradict himself. If we consider Kearns's racial philosophy in light of the previously discussed ideologies of Africanized slavery, we recognize Kearns's statements as entirely consistent with each other. Kearns does not feel dual sympathies for social justice and black slavery's afterlife; he in fact perceives them as fundamentally compatible with one another. Like other white

---

50. J. C. Kearns, *The Life of Blessed Martin De Porres: Saintly American Negro and Patron of Social Justice*, 194; Norbert Georges, *With Blessed Martin De Porres: Favorite Stories from The Torch* (New York: Blessed Martin Guild, 1944), 42; I avoid the smoother-sounding term "mixed race" because of the way in which in Peru and I argue throughout the Americas, "mestizaje works differently for blacks versus Indians." Tanya Maria Golash-Boza, *Yo Soy Negro: Blackness in Peru* (Gainesville: University Press of Florida, 2011), 10
51. Kearns, *Life of Blessed Martin de Porres*, 43.
52. Ibid., 66.

Catholics, he misunderstands not just the relation between slavery and racism but also the definition of slavery itself. Kearns seemingly believes the church can be an overseer and a freedom fighter all at once.

Other twentieth-century admirers similarly perceived Porres through the cracked glass of antiblackness supremacy. Attributing his conversion from admitted racist to advocate for racial justice to Porres' example, the white Dominican priest Thomas McGlynn sculpted a statue of him and wrote a widely distributed pamphlet about his life. However, like Kearns, McGlynn unfortunately promoted Porres to the masses at least in part for the way Porres purportedly proved that "the only intelligent attitude toward racial persecution is the same as the only sensible outlook on any sort of suffering—Christian patience," which, he explained, emerged only as "a product of faith and humility."[53] Why does McGlynn's theory of suffering enable antiblackness? Although patience can be an expression of virtue, it is not the right response to every set of circumstances. And, when prescribed by whites to blacks, it almost always functions as a strategy of pacification.

This holds especially true given that McGlynn proposes black patience as a distinctly Christian virtue. If Christ models Christian patience on the cross, then McGlynn's counsel suggests that black people should wait for either their white crucifiers to pull out the nails they have driven into black people's hands and feet, or another set of heroic white bystanders to somehow intervene and execute a racial rescue. Given McGlynn's passion for both Porres in particular and black evangelization in general, it seems that his affinity for black patience reflects less an expectation that white racists would be reformed and more a desire to play the role of white hero and savior. While McGlynn most likely did in fact desire that black people someday make it down from their crosses, he advised them to do so only under someone else's power. Here again, black independence and fugitivity appear more un-Christian than black suffering. Because he believed that black life

53. Cussen, *Black Saint of the Americas*, 192.

ought to be contingent on the wills of white people, McGlynn upheld the afterlife of black slavery even as he intended to advocate for racial justice.

Slavery's afterlife inhabited the minds of even the white Dominican nun Leo Marie Preher, who sincerely believed that Porres could help to model the solution to what she described as "the race problem." She turned to him for two reasons: he instructed white people to love everyone regardless of race and inspired black people to follow his example of holy patience and suffering. To this end, her 1941 dissertation praised "Blessed Martin" for his "utter absence of what is the root of impatience, namely, the feeling that there was anything due to him." So he "inspired [black slaves] with patience to endure their sufferings," by travelling "each morning . . . go to the negroes of the surrounding sections . . . ministering to their bodies [and] instructing them in Christian doctrine."[54] Preher unwittingly describes a slave master's fantasy: voluntarily submissive black slaves. She further affirms proslavery ideologies by casting an enslaved person as morally good when she submits to her master and evil when she rebels or flees.

The theological implications of Porres' sainthood in fact conflict with Preher's commitment to human rights as a political good. In this same text, she forcefully insists that "the only panacea for the manifestations of racial prejudice is an admission by each member of the dominant group that the negro has rights which are denied him."[55] More than simply sanctioning the bad racial habits already present in white Catholics, Porres' sainthood can in fact prevent emerging good habits from bearing theological fruit. Her belief that Porres can solve "the race problem" also distorts her definition of it. Because he loved, served, and sought relationship with every class of person, Porres opposes what Preher identifies as the evil of "racial discrimination." Like many of her white contemporaries, Preher categorizes this relatively timeless injustice as one that many different types of people experienced and one that many different types of

54. Sr. Leo Marie Preher, *The Social Implications in the Work of Blessed Martin de Porres* (Washington, DC: Catholic University of America Press, 1941), 37.
55. Ibid., 121.

people seemed to inflict. According to Preher, in the contemporary United States, "there is prejudice against recent immigrants, especially those from South Europe, [as well as] against Mexicans and Orientals, against Jews and Negroes." And in Porres' Peru, mulattos were not just victims of racial hatred but also perpetrators of it: they "despised" Spaniards as well as "negroes." Nearly anyone could be the victim of racial prejudice, just as nearly anyone could be the perpetrator of it.[56] If Porres' ministry provides the answer, then it also supplies the question.

The ambivalent racial status of mixed-raced people plays an essential role in Preher's racial theology. Perhaps unwittingly echoing the interpretive strategies of Porres' early hagiographers Cipriano and Bernardo de Medina, Preher argues that Porres's mulatto body makes him an example that both whites and blacks ought to follow. Porres served as a role model for contemporary black people because, even though the Spaniards presumably hated him for being a mulatto, he did not hate the Spaniards in return; he qualified as a role model for contemporary whites because of his refusal to hate darker-skinned blacks, as Preher claimed other mulattos did. Pursuing what Preher described as "harmonious relations between all races," Porres offered racial healing not just to his own society but to Preher's as well.[57] If Porres loved even enslaved blacks, then surely Anglo-Saxon Americans could love Hungarian immigrants and Russian Jews as well. And if Porres loved the cruel Spaniards, then surely African Americans could love even the most bigoted white man or woman.

But racial evil does not operate uniformly against all non-white peoples. Antiblackness supremacy in particular emerges from the afterlife of slavery, and slavery oppresses its victims not by

56. Father John La Farge offers a similar understanding of racial prejudice when he argues that "race prejudice . . . is not entirely confined to the dominant group. Every social tendency produces a reaction, and it would be strange if white prejudice against the Negro were not met by a certain degree of Negro prejudice against the white. While the form that such anti-white prejudice takes is the mild one of distrust and suspicion rather than of aggression, its presence is one of the complications of interracial relations" (John La Farge, *The Race Question and the Negro: A Study of the Catholic Doctrine on Interracial Justice* [New York: Longmans, Green, 1937], 183).
57. Preher, *Social Implications*, 67. For another example of this hagiographical trope, see Georges, *With Blessed Martin de Porres*, 16, 72.

discriminating against them, refusing intimacy with them, or failing to live harmoniously with them. Slavery mistreats its victims by plunging them into a state of social death and natal alienation that is maintained by structural as well as interpersonal violence. Just as Claver's does, Porres' sainthood encourages Catholics to misunderstand both racial evil in general and antiblackness supremacy in particular. More than simply limiting Catholic capacity to dismantle antiblackness supremacy, their sainthoods in fact fortify it.

7.5 Porres and Twentieth-Century Catholic Racial Triumphalism

The church similarly has enlisted Porres's memory in order to spin a tale of ecclesial racial innocence and heroism. In this way, a group of white Dominican priests founded the Blessed Martin Guild in New York City in 1935 in order "to erase the impression among non-white people that the Catholic church is not Catholic but only Western-White."[58] Deeming these impressions to be a misunderstanding rather than an accurate assessment of reality, these priests believed they could correct them by adding a black face to the church's predominantly white canon.[59]

Just as Catholic clerics used Claver's sainthood to advance a Catholic racial triumphalism over and against Protestants, during the 1930s, church leaders championed the cause of Porres's canonization in order not just to "attract blacks to Catholicism" but also to "keep them out of the hands of atheists, Protestants, secularists, socialists, and communists."[60] A member of the Blessed Martin Guild, the white Dominican priest and professor Ignatius Smith articulated an especially emphatic form of Catholic racial triumphalism: he proclaimed that "the new Negro of the United States will find no rest, no peace, no solace, and no happiness in godless indifference." In atheism "the new Negro" would "find only chains more harrowing than those of the slavery of the past in the promises of communism."

58. Cussen, *Black Saint of the Americas*, 193.
59. For a brief overview of the history of Catholic attempts to use Porres as a tool of black evangelization, see Georges, *With Blessed Martin de Porres*, 66–69.
60. Cussen, *Black Saint of the Americas*, 195.

So would derive "only a fleeting joy in the emotionally appeals of passing and man-made [presumably Protestant] religions."[61] An aristocratic Russian immigrant named Catherine de Hueck similarly opened a friendship house and named it after Porres because she believed it would disprove the Communist Party's claim that "they have the only solution of the race problem." Some black Catholics agreed. In this way, the founding member and president of a coalition of black Catholic parishes called the Saint Martín de Porres Retreat League, a woman known only as Mrs. Cook explained, "We feel like that under the patronage of Blessed Martin we can do our bit in bringing about the conversion of the Negro race to Catholicism."[62]

Another black Catholic, a prominent member of the Federated Colored Catholics named Gustave B. Aldrich, initially appeared to echo the hagiographical arguments of Porres's champions when he stressed that the dearth of black Catholic saints had led black Catholic children "to the conclusion that their own people never did anything along the line of religion." But in truth he unsettled dominant hagiographical narratives when he argued that "the representation of black saints and great men of the faith in our Catholic colored churches will go far to rehabilitating our self-respect and will also gain for us the sincere admiration and regard of the white Catholics." More pointedly, he added that the elevation of a black saint like Porres would "take away some of the sting of the supercilious and scornful remarks of negro non-Catholics, who sometimes . . . charge us with servile subservience in religion to the white people."[63]

While white church leaders proposed Porres in order to repair the reputation of the church, Aldrich instead prioritized the reputation of black Catholics. But Aldrich did not express concern for the way black Catholics might appear to white audiences. He instead privileged the perceptions that black people had of both each other and themselves. In this way, Aldrich insisted that the elevation of black saints would "go far to rehabilitate [black Catholics'] self-respect." With this focus,

61. Georges, *With Blessed Martin de Porres*, 41.
62. Cussen, *Black Saint of the Americas*, 195.
63. Ibid., 190.

Aldrich both unveiled and attempted to unravel the alliance between the Catholic hagiographical imagination and regnant ideologies of racialized slavery. Thus, while Porres's mostly white and Dominican champions presented his canonization as a way to increase the number of black people who belonged to the Catholic Church, Aldrich urged his canonization in order to express black power: he urged the church to submit to "the demands [of black Catholics] for Negro statues of Negro saints."[64]

Aldrich spoke the language not of black gratitude or white paternalistic outreach but of black power and black rights. He referenced what black people were owed by pointing to what they demanded. In so doing, he discredits slavery's core logic: according to the slave master, his slaves are owed nothing and must be given everything. Rather than making demands for what they lack, slaves ought to express gratitude for what they have received. The logic of white mastership also claimed to already know what black people wanted and needed; there was no reason to let black people speak for themselves. In revealing that black Catholics neither admired nor felt affection toward white Catholics, Aldrich struck at the heart of one of slavery and its afterlife's most cherished lies: that black people were grateful for white people. In making this dislike public, Aldrich also perhaps subtly hinted at the possibility of black rebellion. To many, it perhaps even sounded like a threat.

Aldrich's subversive approach to hagiography unfortunately could not counteract white dominance within the church. The hagiographical alliance between antiblackness supremacy and Catholic racial triumphalism persisted into the 1960s. The white Jesuit racial reformer John La Farge continued to favor Porres due to the fact that although "his Negro-Indian mother conceived him out of wedlock" and "that his proud Spanish father . . . disliked him for his Negroid appearance," Porres' heart was turned to not "rebellion and bitterness" but humility.[65] Porres therefore offered "that type of active

64. Ibid.
65. John La Farge, "The Humility of Martin de Porres," *Interracial Review* 35 (September 1962): 205.

witness which we desperately need for our own present time and circumstances" because he can change the mind of "the American Negro," whom he lamented "at the present is less and less inclined to relish praise for being humble." As if anticipating an objection from an increasingly militant audience, La Farge admitted that "the praise of humility . . . can be perverted into praise of injustice," but he insisted that Saint Martín modeled a different sort of humility, one that overturns injustice.[66]

According to La Farge, black people who critiqued his canonization simply misunderstood him. La Farge defended the holiness of Porres' humility on the grounds that he "freely chose the humble career to which he dedicated himself." La Farge even attempted to present Porres as a civil rights leader, arguing that he embodied a "spirit . . . no different from the spirit of decent, God-fearing people in the United States who stand up for their own and their neighbor's civil rights." La Farge's analogy initially appears incoherent: one rightly wonders how Porres's passive nonresistance to racial abuse in any way resembles the black civil rights movement's commitment to actively defying it. But in truth, what seems to be a logical error in fact reveals a deeper insight. La Farge perceives Porres as a civil rights fighter because he perceives both types of people as nonviolent. But La Farge's love for black pacifism is perverse. Like other white racial reformers, La Farge placed undue stress on nonviolence when assessing black morality and holiness.

In truth, the black civil rights movement differs from Porres' way of living much more than it resembles it. Porres endured racial cruelty as an end in itself; activists in the black civil rights movement subjected themselves to racial cruelty in order to denounce it. There is simply no evidence that Porres wished to change the racial order; to the contrary, he enforced it. If the civil rights movement sometimes provoked violence against black people in order to unveil it as evil, then Porres promoted and participated in violence against black people in order to illuminate it as God's will for them.

66. Ibid., 206.

La Farge continued to espouse a Catholic racial triumphalism, interpreting black history as evidence of the church's superiority. La Farge perhaps aimed to represent Porres as a Spanish-speaking Martin Luther King Jr. in order to dispel what he believed to be the myth that the civil rights movement proved that black-led Protestant churches served black people's interests better than the white-led Catholic church did. In response, La Farge wished to prove that black people could find fulfillment only through Catholicism: the black civil rights movement is a poor imitation of what the Catholic Church had been doing for black people for four centuries. In his view, "the natural humility of the Negro," which expressed itself in black people's "remarkable . . . patience and cheerfulness under the whiplash of prideful scorn," made black people and the Catholic church a perfect match.[67] Only the white-led Catholic church could bring black people's "natural humility" to its supernatural end. Whether La Farge believed that blacks' humility predated their enslavement and therefore helped to explain it or whether their humility had simply resulted from enslavement, he does not say.

Interpreted charitably, La Farge attempted to redirect black humility away from white masters and toward God. Even if we accept this more flattering account, we nonetheless ought to reject it. In practice, white servility to God has always meant co-mastership with God while black servility to God instead ends up justifying enslavement to both white people and God. White people have never really been slaves to God, just as they have never truly acted as slaves to other human beings. La Farge ultimately perceives black people as prizes that white people win. Expressing this, he asked, "What could be more appealing to the Catholic zeal for souls, to Catholic apostolic spirit, than the natural humility of the Negro when this trait is spiritualized and shines like a crown upon the brows of Negro members of the Catholic Church?"[68] The Church he imagines as predominately white is

67. Ibid., 205.
68. Ibid.

owed black converts; the souls of black people belong to them and no one else.

7.6 The Church as Champion of the World

Although the saintly afterlives of Claver and Porres share much in common, Porres's blackness arguably has made him a much more versatile saint. Black slavery and its afterlife treat black people as uniquely fungible. Fungibility refers to the fact that slavery turns enslaved people into the ultimate tools and instruments: they can be used for literally any purpose.[69] For example, throughout history, enslaved people have served as scribes, blacksmiths, soldiers, sex objects, concubines, wives, wet nurses, laborers, oarsmen, ornaments, cooks, and inventors to name just a few. Habituated by its residence in an environment of antiblackness supremacy, the church unsurprisingly has tended to treat both Porres as a fungibile, hagiographical commodity.[70] First, in 1939, the president of Peru declared Porres "a symbol of interracial brotherhood and the solidarity of classes." Pope Pius XII would embrace this title a few years later.[71] In his homily during Porres's 1962 canonization Mass, Pope John XXIII similarly celebrated Porres as "the vindication of all the oppressed of the world."[72] Both of these titles were possible only because of the way that slavery and its afterlife perceives nearly any kind of suffering and oppression as an expression or instance of blackness.

Second, the perceived fungibility of Porres' blackness has enabled the church to use Porres in order to exonerate itself of nearly any crime or error. In 1939, a papal nuncio "underscored the poignancy of the universal reverence for a 'negro' at a time when the world was witnessing Hitler."[73] More than simply "defeating racism," as the nuncio hoped, his canonization would also depict the church as the enemy of the emerging Nazi imperial order. Shortly after Porres's

69. Anthony P. Farley, "The Apogee of the Commodity," *DePaul Law Review* 53 (2004): 1234.
70. Wilderson, *Red, White, and Black*, 58–59; Farley, "Apogee of the Commodity," 1229.
71. Cussen, *Black Saint of the Americas*, 197.
72. Ibid., 202.
73. Ibid., 196.

canonization, the Vatican newspaper, *L'osservatore Romana,* celebrated him for "rising to bear witness to the principles of unity, universalism, and equality that Christianity has affirmed powerfully in the world."[74] The mere fact of Porres' blackness enables him to symbolize the church's struggle against nearly any form of evil, even those in which the church did not actually act heroically. In recognizing Porres's moral goodness, the church can proclaim its own.

What is wrong with these invocations? Precisely because of the way in which slavery's afterlife perceives both black people and blackness as fungible, blackness does not stand alongside that to which it is being compared. The comparison instead consumes it like a parasite feeds off its host, that is, like a master lives off her slave.[75] When the church wields Porres' blackness into an instrument with which to make self-congratulatory analogies, it does not simply obscure the specificity of antiblackness, it undermines black movements for freedom. Why? In addition to erroneously portraying the fight against antiblackness supremacy as a battle that has already been won, this rhetorical strategy casts the church as a combatant that has always been on the right side of this triumphant struggle.

The church does not err by either recognizing that Porres's humanity extends beyond his racial identity or imbuing his sainthood with more than an exclusively racial meaning. No, when the church treats Porres' blackness as an analogy for something else, it skews its understanding of antiblackness; this in turn makes it easier for Catholics to overestimate the extent of our racial progress. In truth, antiblackness supremacy possesses a fundamental uniqueness: since it draws strength from slavery and its afterlife, it does not in fact bear any particular resemblance to other forms of oppression. Like slavery itself, antiblackness supremacy differs from other forms of injustice at least as much as it resembles them. Porres's blackness does not make him a symbol of the exploited worker or the struggle against oppression itself any more than Teresa of Avila's femininity

---

74. Ibid., 202. For other examples of Porres' purportedly healing universality, see Georges, *With Blessed Martin de Porres,* 66.
75. Patterson, *Slavery and Social Death,* 14.

does. Like Preher, contemporary non-black Catholics may recognize that black people have been deprived of certain rights, but we will continue to share her inability to identify both their specific content and the means necessary to secure them until we accept that antiblackness supremacy is uniquely rooted in slavery's afterlife. When nonblack people deploy blackness as an analogy, they do not stand in solidarity with blackness as much as they enlist it in their service.

8

Venerable Pierre Toussaint and the Search for Fugitive Saints

Since both Claver and Porres were canonized in the pre–civil rights era, their racially flawed sainthoods may appear to suggest that the church has participated in antiblackness mainly through its inability to confess its sinful past.[1] Unfortunately, however, the ongoing cause to canonize the nineteenth-century, Haitian-born, black New Yorker Pierre Toussaint reveals that the church has not simply inherited bad hagiographical habits; it continues to enact them even in the present. Toussaint's campaign suggests this due to the four following facts: first, his first white supporters were from the city of New York, which abolished slavery in the relatively early year of 1800; second, he was not rediscovered until the early 1940s, when a young white seminarian stumbled upon his story while doing some research; third, unlike the causes of Claver and Porres, which were first pushed along by elites who inhabited a society deeply reliant upon slave holding, Toussaint's cause was championed by groups like the John Boyle O'Reilly

---

1. Prusak, "Theological Considerations—Hermeneutical, Ecclesiological, Eschatological."

Committee for Interracial Justice, which existed to advance the cause of racial justice for black people.[2] The cause to canonize Toussaint sheds an unflattering light on the contemporary church for a fourth reason: his canonization process was not officially initiated until 1951, nearly one hundred years after slavery's bloody abolition, and he was not proclaimed venerable until 1996, more than four full decades after the United States Supreme Court declared racial segregation unconstitutional.

The afterlife of slavery is not a mere echo within the church's hagiographical imagination like some faint reminder of a far-distant past. The church still struggles to define black holiness in a way that defies the logic of Africanized slavery and its afterlife. The intentions of his advocates notwithstanding, the cause to canonize Toussaint upholds the afterlife of slavery in both the church and the world.

8.1 Toussaint as Saint of Counterrevolutionary Order

In the United States, the hagiographical narrative used to propel Toussaint's canonization process forward comes largely from the 1854 biography written by the white, U.S.–American best-selling novelist Hannah Farnham Sawyer Lee. Her account was adapted by various Catholic authors in the twentieth century for explicitly religious purposes. Due to their connection to the canonization process, this chapter therefore focuses primarily on these sources.

Toussaint's initial hagiographical renown derived primarily from his gentlemanly service to his white mistress. He placed her needs above even his own, and he continued to tend to her long after he could have been free. His late-twentieth- and early-twenty-first century advocates portray him as an inspiration to black people due to his extraordinary piety and rise to fame, fortune, and high-class status in an otherwise racist city. Both groups of admirers acclaim his extraordinary piety and love for not all just all people but also the Catholic Church.

As occurs with the sainthoods of Claver and Porres, Toussaint's

2. Arthur Jones, *Pierre Toussaint: A Biography* (New York: Doubleday Religion, 2003), 2; R. Jackson, "Plaque Honors 18th Century New York Man," *Indianapolis Recorder*, July 21, 1951.

hagiographical alignment with slavery's afterlife grows even more apparent when read in light of its historical context. And, although they would disagree with my critique of him, Toussaint's hagiographers share my sense of history's importance to the story of his holiness. In this way, nineteenth- and twentieth-century hagiographers alike both dwell extensively on the Haitian Revolution that Toussaint's master fled. Narrating the Revolution in significant detail, they describe those who fought it as brutal, murderous, chaotic, disobedient, and disorderly. For example, according to the 1979 hagiography written by the New Jersey–born white priest Boniface Hanley, the Revolution exploded into "an orgy of vicious crime and reprisal"; the island's black revolutionaries "hid in the countryside and formed ravaging bands which attacked the unwary; they burned, pillaged, and raped."[3] Toussaint's hagiographers are right to emphasize this history: Toussaint's reputation as a saint does not make sense without it. Nearly every aspect of the standard hagiographical story about Toussaint aims to portray him the exact opposite of his revolutionary countrywomen and men: he was tranquil, docile, orderly, and most of all, obedient to his mistress.

In order to exalt Toussaint as a saint of counterrevolutionary order, his hagiographers describe Toussaint's owners, a married couple known as the Bérards, as unjustly victimized by Revolution.[4] Why? Hagiographers make sure to differentiate the Bérards from other slave owners, noting that while other Haitian masters cruelly forced their slaves to toil in unforgiving sugarcane fields, the Bérards treated Toussaint to a life of ease and comfort as a house slave. They even taught him how to read. According to Hanley, "Berard treated his slaves with genuine respect."[5] Although other slave owners may have deserved to lose life and property in the revolution, the Bérards did not.[6] Thus even when hagiographers condemn certain aspects of

---

3. Boniface Hanley, *Ten Christians: By Their Deeds You Shall Known Them* (Notre Dame, IN: Ave Maria Press, 1979), 22.
4. Here I borrow from the filmmaker Ezra Edelman, who described O. J. Simpson as "a counterrevolutionary athlete" in his film series *O. J.: Made in America*, ESPN.com, accessed December 5, 2016, http://tinyurl.com/z44je26.
5. Hanley, *Ten Christians*, 18.

Haitian slavery as Hanley does, they do so ultimately to excuse not just the Bérards but slavery itself.[7] Precisely because this narrative strategy portrays slavery as only circumstantially rather than inherently unjust, it also casts the revolution as at least as immoral as the evil it opposed. It also implicitly condemns these revolutionaries for their purportedly refusing to distinguish between "good" slave owners and bad ones.[8]

After detailing the perceived horrors of the Haitian Revolution, Toussaint's hagiographical script picks up immediately upon his master and mistress' arrival in New York City. Confident that Haiti's black insurrection would soon be defeated, the Bérards believed their respite in New York would be short-lived. For this reason, the family patriarch, Jean Bérard, returned to Haiti in order to check on his property.[9] Shortly after discovering that his land had been destroyed, Bérard fell ill and died before he could return to New York. Hagiographers describe both events as great tragedies. Widowed and no longer wealthy, Madame Bérard appears especially pitiful.[10] For this reason, Toussaint's devotion to her qualifies as not servile but saintly. Although his training as hair stylist to New York's rich and famous had made him rich and famous himself, Toussaint did not seize upon his mistress's misfortune as an occasion to purchase his own freedom. Laudably, Toussaint instead "chose to continue as her slave when he had every right to be free."[11] He exceeded his duty: more than simply "leaving no bills unpaid," he "spent not one penny on himself until all necessities and little luxuries for the Bérard household were obtained"; he dedicated all of his extra money to her luxury and all of his extra time "to cheering her up."[12] As Hanley explains, "Madame Berard was his first concern."[13] Reportedly "wishing for no

6. For more examples of this hagiographical trope, see Ellen Terry, *The Other Toussaint: A Post-Revolutionary Black* (Boston: Daughters of St. Paul, 1981), 8, 11–13.
7. Hanley, *Ten Christians*, 18.
8. Hanley also speaks of "the poor woman's woes" (ibid., 23).
9. Ibid., 22.
10. Terry, *Other Toussaint*, 114.
11. Hanley, *Ten Christians*, 25.
12. Ibid., 22. As of December 5, 2016, an excerpt from this book remains available for viewing on the website of the popular Catholic media organization EWTN, at http://tinyurl.com/gne8xse.

return" from his mistress, he refused ever to accept her gratitude.[14] According to Lee, when his mistress attempted to thank him for his life of service, he sounded almost astonished, replying, "O Madame! I have only done my duty." Toussaint asked for nothing except the opportunity to fulfill his duty: in this way, he professed that he "only asked to make her comfortable, and I bless God that she never knew a want."[15] Her happiness was his own: "some of his happiest moments came when he could set her hair and dress it in the very latest fashion."[16] Seemingly possessing no desires of his own, he "endeavored to procure for her little offerings of taste . . . not because they had any specific value for himself, but simply for the pleasure that they gave to her."[17]

Even after his mistress remarried another Frenchman, surnamed Nicholas, Toussaint continued to place his mistress first. Although Toussaint fell in love with "a young, black Haitian girl named Juliette Noel," he "felt that he could not marry [her] while he still bore responsibilities for the Nicolas household."[18] Prioritizing his former mistress's family above his own even after her death had freed him, "Toussaint remained with her [second] husband" and "continued . . . to perform many gratuitous services" for him.[19]

Some may interrupt at this point and claim that the purportedly voluntary character of Toussaint's service makes him more Christ-like than servile. But rather than departing from the ideology of slaveocracy, the voluntary character of Toussaint's servitude fulfills its deepest fantasy. Toussaint's purportedly desiring only what his mistress did and skillfully attending to her obeys slavery's logic perfectly. Consider the following anecdote about a time when, shortly

13. Hanley, *Ten Christians*, 25. For more examples of this hagiographical trope, see Terry, *Other Toussaint*, 106.
14. Hannah Farnham Sawyer Lee, *Memoir of Pierre Toussaint, Born a Slave in St. Domingo* (Boston: Crosby, Nichols, Lee & Co., 1854), 23.
15. Ibid., 27. For more about Lee, see Maria Carla Sanchez, *Reforming the World: Social Activism and the Problem of Fiction in Nineteenth Century America* (Iowa City: University of Iowa Press, 2009), 34, 73–85.
16. Hanley, *Ten Christians*, 26.
17. Lee, *Memoir of Pierre Toussaint*, 26. For more descriptions of Toussaint's devotion to his mistress and master's pleasure, see Terry, *Other Toussaint*, 101.
18. Hanley, *Ten Christians*, 29.
19. Lee, *Memoir of Pierre Toussaint*, 31.

after he arrived in the United States, "the free negroes and some of the Quakers tried to persuade [Toussaint] to leave his mistress," telling him that "freedom was his own right." Repudiating them, Toussaint declared, "[My freedom] . . . belongs to my mistress."[20] Ultimately, Toussaint flattered the religious sensibilities of his white friends precisely for his willingness to perform his servile duties as though they were gifts. In so doing, he portrayed the bonds that tie slave to master as not violently coercive but gratuitous and loving.

The purportedly voluntary character of Toussaint's devotion to his white mistress proves especially well suited to his particular historical context. More than simply eroding white people's confidence that their slaves loved them, the Haitian Revolution suggested that their slaves might actually hate them. White people had always feared that their slaves would try to kill them; in the wake of the Haitian Revolution, interracial proximity likely had never felt so terrifying. Epitomizing fidelity to the lives of white folks, Toussaint helped to soothe these anxieties. As if in response to dispatches from the Haitian Revolution's white refugees who churned out sensationalized stories about black men raping white women and girls, Toussaint loved white women intensely but in a decidedly nonsexual fashion.[21] He dreamed only "of the mountains of tiered curls he had fashioned during the course of a day."[22] As if repudiating the black Haitian revolutionaries who claimed freedom as a right, Toussaint would accept it only as a gift. And as if denouncing those self-emancipated black women and men who valued their freedom more than the lives of their masters, Toussaint cherished his mistress's life and comfort above his freedom. Each of these traits upholds counterrevolutionary racial order.

If the Haitian Revolution was both disorderly and disordered, then Toussaint restored order, both literally and symbolically. In this way, anecdotes about Toussaint's tidiness help to comprise his

20. Ibid., 85.
21. Gerald Home, *Confronting Black Jacobins: The U.S., the Haitian Revolution, and the Dominican Republic* (New York: New York University Press, 2015), 53; David Patrick Greggus, *The World of the Haitian Revolution* (Bloomington: Indiana University Press, 2009), 255.
22. Terry, *Other Toussaint*, 106.

hagiographical renown. To this end, he is described as "dressing in the most neat and proper manner" and "arranging . . . [his house] with an air of neatness." So his similarly wife "made his house pleasant to him . . . by her neatness and order." Above all, "the neatness and order of their household was striking."[23] Even these seemingly trivial characteristics serve a racially ideological purpose.

More than simply ending slavery, the Haitian Revolution overturned social order by violently asserting not only black rights to freedom, but also black power over white bodies and property. According to the logic of racialized slavery, only white men could rape black women with impunity.[24] The Haitian Revolution, at least in the minds of white observers, established a world in which black men could rape white women. Toussaint returned sexual relations to right racial order. More than simply lacking any discernable desire to have sex with white women, Toussaint's hair-dressing skills affirmed the white-supremacist aesthetic that placed white femininity at the pinnacle of human beauty. Instead of despoiling the purity of white femininity, as rapist Haitian revolutionaries purportedly did, Toussaint ensured that it remained intact.[25] His hairstyling skills made white women beautiful.

Further restoring counterrevolutionary order, although Toussaint took care of his white mistress and his wealthy white female clients, he did not exercise authority over them. He loved white women not as a father but a servant. But he did not relinquish his right to exercise masculine authority over all women. He acted as paternal caretaker and authority figure to his black wife, a woman named Juliette, whom hagiographies describe as "childlike," "twenty years younger than he," and also "always yielding to Toussaint's [will], because she said she was not obliged to do it."[26] He also served as a doting uncle to Euphemia, the niece he adopted after his sister died. As a servant to white women

23. Hagiographers also describe Toussaint as literally orderly: Lee, *Memoir of Pierre Toussaint*, 25, 48, 80, 82.
24. DuBois, *Avengers of the New World*, 47.
25. Lee, *Memoir of Pierre Toussaint*, 16–17, 34–35, 74, 121.
26. Ibid., 53.

and a father to black women, Toussaint appeared to uphold social hierarchy of both race and sex.

Toussaint's appeal perhaps also derives from his lack of biological children and familial connections to other men. Toussaint had only two family members: his young wife, who died before she could reach middle age, and his niece, who died shortly after turning fourteen. According to the patriarchal and patrilineal rules that structured life in the antebellum United States, a man could not pass his name, property, or power on to his wife and daughters as he could to his sons. As a natally alienated slave, Toussaint had already been excised from ordinary chains of inheritance and filiation. His lack of male heirs ensured that he would remain outside of these processes of paternity even after his emancipation.[27] Even his freedom he received from a woman.

Toussaint further soothed the counterrevolutionary psyche by rejecting not just violent black rebellion but abolitionism itself. When a woman asked him if he was an abolitionist, he reportedly "shuddered, and replied, '[The abolitionists] have never seen blood flow as I have,'" and "then added, 'They don't know what they are doing.'"[28] In this way, Toussaint assured white people both that their fears about black people were valid and that they were unlikely to come true. More than simply rebuking abolitionists, many of whom were pacifists, he argued that black freedom, when acquired by right rather than as a gift, would inevitably unleash unspeakable violence. In so doing, he cast white mastership as a prerequisite to survival and a form of self-defense. At least as portrayed in hagiographies, Toussaint vindicates white mastership even as a freeman.[29] When black New Yorkers invited Toussaint to march in a parade celebrating the recent abolition of slavery, he declined, explaining, "I do not owe my freedom to the State, but to my mistress." Toussaint insisted that he was free neither by right nor by will but only by the gratuitous and un-coerced will of his mistress. Uttering a counterrevolutionary rebuke, Toussaint

27. Ibid., 99.
28. Ibid., 85.
29. Hartman, *Scenes of Subjection*, 130–34.

reportedly insisted that "no failure on the part of the master can absolve a slave from his duty."[30] He refuted the Haitian Revolution in its entirety.

Further restoring counterrevolutionary order, Toussaint also knew his place, both literally and figuratively. Consider the following exchange between Toussaint and a white friend. Toussaint fondly recalled how he would take his young black niece, Euphemia, with him to pass out "buns, jumbles, and gingerbread" to the residents of the Catholic Orphan School for white children. Somewhat alarmed, his white friend asked, "You let her give them to the children?" Seemingly incredulous that his friend would doubt his racial decorum, Toussaint responded, "O, no, madam! That would not be proper for the little black girl." Toussaint instead instructed Euphemia to "ask one of the sisters if she will give [the goodies] to the children." The two of them would "stand on one side" of the schoolyard in order to observe the white children's joy from afar.[31] Toussaint does not simply privilege white people's joy above his own; white people's joy *is* his own.

Toussaint also knew his place in a figurative sense. According to one hagiographer, Toussaint did "not appear to have entertained any inordinate desire for his own freedom." He instead "was fulfilling his duty in the situation in which his Heavenly Father chose to place him, and that idea gave him peace and serenity."[32] Here, God's will, natural duty, and the slave's happiness all seem one and the same. According to his hagiographers, Toussaint did not simply accept his divinely ordained slavery and perform its duties; he did so peacefully. Toussaint's peaceful submission portrays racial hierarchy as the fulfillment of a natural order perfectly designed by God rather than the result of the violent and arbitrary assertion of human will. Toussaint appears to be the perfect slave.

Precisely because he enacted an extremely pious form of black Catholic servility, Toussaint perhaps also helped to make New York City's French Catholic residents feel secure in a world unsettled by

30. Lee, *Memoir of Pierre Toussaint*, 56.
31. Ibid., 52.
32. Ibid., 57.

three revolutions: the Haitian, the French, and the American. Especially when contrasted with certain strands of political thought inspired by the Enlightenment and the Protestant Reformation, the Catholic imagination—even when racially neutral—tended to hold a relatively favorable evaluation of social, ecclesial, and political hierarchy.[33] The revolutionary fervors that swept across the United States, Haiti, and France in the late eighteenth century may have posed particular psychological and philosophical challenges to these Catholics.[34] While the French Revolution had challenged the supremacy of Catholicism, kings, and aristocrats, the Haitian Revolution had upended the supremacy of whiteness.[35] Intensifying their disorientation, these white exiles to New York also had found racial refuge in an overwhelmingly Protestant nation that had just experienced a revolution of its own. In knowing his place, Toussaint helped New York's white Frenchwomen and -men find theirs as well. Toussaint signaled to them that one could still be Catholic, wealthy, and white-supremacist even in a kingless, Protestant country such as the United States.

More than simply vindicating the social order that had been shattered by Haiti's black revolutionaries, Toussaint helped New York's white French-speaking refugees adapt to a new one. While Toussaint's career as a hairdresser may have begun in the homes of Frenchwomen, he quickly gained an impressive array of white Anglo-Saxon Protestant clients and friends, including heavyweights such as the Schuylers. In this way, Toussaint served to reconcile already established English-speaking Protestant white women elites with the French and Catholic newcomers.[36] Smoothing away the rough edges of potential ethno-religious conflict, Toussaint helped to fashion a unified white racial and economic elite. In contrast to those Haitian revolutionaries unsettled

33. Maura Jane Farrelly, "American Slavery, American Freedom, American Catholicism," *Early American Studies: An Interdisciplinary Journal* 10, no. 1 (2012): 72, 75–76. John T. McGreevy, *Catholicism and American Freedom: A History* (New York: Norton, 2003), 12–15.

34. Owen White, *In God's Empire: French Missionaries in the Modern World* (New York: Oxford University Press, 2012), 7–8; Ashli White, *Encountering Revolution: Haiti and the Making of the Early Republic* (Baltimore, MD: Johns Hopkins University Press, 2010), 2–5.

35. Hanley, *Ten Christians*, 28.

36. Lee, *Memoir of Pierre Toussaint*, 69, 127.

who burned the land their former masters once had owned rather than submitting it to the principles of profit maximization, Toussaint was renowned for his extraordinary frugality.[37] Unlike the revolutionaries who wasted the land and therefore threw their wealth away, Toussaint exhibited an exceptional capacity to save his money. In this way, the exemplar of Catholic piety often appears more like a poster boy for the Protestant work ethic.

Toussaint's reputation for avoiding debt further enabled these white New Yorkers to maintain their racial position in an era of economic transition.[38] The ideology of slavery envisions the slave as a person who does not simply labor in the service of an unrepayable debt but whose very life qualifies as such. Toussaint enforces the rule of ontologically indebted blackness by appearing the represent its exception. Put another way, Toussaint's frugality and entrepreneurial success portrayed indebtedness as a characteristic that all black people shared but virtuous individuals could overcome. In an era of increasing industrialization, Toussaint affirmed an ideology in which men possessed credit and capital due not to structural advantages but as a result of individual moral discipline. Especially in the nineteenth-century United States, Toussaint's racialized semiotics of debt also hid both how white people purchased black slaves primarily only if they could afford to go into debt, and how black people themselves were the credit that helped to fuel the United States's nineteenth-century economic rise.[39] As read through the lens of Toussaint's life story, whiteness appears as an achievement of virtue rather than violence.

8.2 What's Love Got to Do with It? Catholic Theology and Racialized Slave Mastership

Like hagiographers of Claver and Porres, Toussaint's hagiographers depict him as universally beloved. This aspect of Toussaint's renown

---

37. DuBois, *Avengers of the New World*, 266, 273, 283.
38. Lee, *Memoir of Pierre Toussaint*, 26.
39. Edward E. Baptist, *The Half Has Never Been Told: Slavery and the Making of American Capitalism* (Philadelphia: Basic Books, 2014), 12, 37, 185, 247, 257, 285–86, 353.

may appear unquestionably good. But in a world marred by antiblackness supremacy, racial virtue undoubtedly would have grated against the grain of common sense. In interpreting Toussaint's popularity as evidence of his holiness, the church presumes that white people perceive moral reality accurately rather than in accordance with their own biases. How can we trust the judgments of the well-bred white people who played an outsized role in spreading his story? Consider Lee's claim that Toussaint served as "a fast and true friend to . . . his own people of color." How can she know this when she admits to excluding black people's testimonies from her biographical data?[40]

Lee ultimately perceived Toussaint as a friend to everyone precisely because he was especially friendly to "those to whose houses he daily resorted . . . the people in New York of the highest class in rank, cultivation, and wealth."[41] As if making a preferential option for the rich and white, Lee suggests that one best loves the poor and black and loving the rich and white most. Rather than locked in structural conflict with each other, Lee imagines whites and blacks as simply inhabiting distinct places within a perfectly aligned organic whole. Lee claims that black New Yorkers loved Toussaint for a second reason: he modeled "what [black people] may become by treading in his footsteps." Lee regrettably implies that black people uniformly aspired to earn the approval of whites. She also depicts blackness as a condition that black people wished to escape and whiteness as the trait they wished to emulate.

As a foil to the revolution that his master and mistress fled, Toussaint helped New York's French- and English-speaking white elite to repair the holes the Haitian Revolution had ripped through the fabric of their racialized universe. Responding strategically to threats against their violently enforced supremacy over black people, these white New Yorkers turned Toussaint into a saint of counterrevolutionary order. They exuberantly embraced a black person whom they perceived as the exception to the rules of blackness

40. Lee, *Memoir of Pierre Toussaint*, 73.
41. Ibid.

precisely because an increasing number of black people no longer followed them. Toussaint received admission to the otherwise all-white club of gentleman primarily because he remained within the performative limits of servile blackness. He qualified as an exception to the rule of ungentlemanly blackness only because he embodied what white people attempted to enforce as the rule. Racialized double standards of virtue prevailed: white men qualified as gentlemen when they displayed mastership of themselves and others while black men were classified as uncivilized when they refused to be mastered by others.

8.3 Toussaint and White Desires for Ecclesial Exoneration

Especially during the end of the twentieth and the start of the twenty-first centuries, the cause for Toussaint's sainthood also has helped to fulfill white desires for individual and ecclesial exoneration. Consider the 1992 defense offered by Thomas J. Wenski, the white priest who served as the director of Miami's Pierre Toussaint Haitian-Catholic Center. In response to black Catholic scholar Albert Raboteau's describing Toussaint as "passive and servile," Wenski argued that John Paul II "is pushing" for Toussaint's canonization due not to his servility but to the fact that "he could still love the church, warts and all."[42] While some enslaved black people may have loved the Catholic Church despite its racial sins, they ought not to be elevated to sainthood for this love alone. Let us return to a metaphor employed when discussing Claver. What would we say if our local social club or civic organization bestowed a medal on a kidnapping victim not because she survived or kept up hope for rescue or displayed any other virtue but because she loved her captors and chose not leave them? What if we discovered that some prominent members in that club or organization were

---

42. Deborah Sontag, "Canonizing a Slave: Saint or Uncle Tom?," *New York Times*, February 23, 1992. Not all black Catholic scholars agreed with Raboteau, however. In his 2004 review of Arthur Jones's biography of Toussaint, the eminent historian Cyprian Davis strongly refuted the notion that Toussaint was "a Catholic Uncle Tom." "Venerable Immigrant," *America Magazine*, February 9, 2004. http://www.americamagazine.org/issue/culture/venerable-immigrant. Accessed December 13, 2016.

among her kidnappers? Rather than passing judgment on the sentiments of any enslaved person, including Toussaint, my critique falls only on those who promote Toussaint's cause.

The cause to canonize Toussaint ought to provoke further discomfort in us due the way that white Catholics struggle to advocate for his cause in ways that do not promote antiblackness supremacy. Consider then archbishop Cardinal John O'Connor of New York's 1993 attempt to prove that "it's time to take Pierre Toussaint seriously." As if echoing the hagiographical assessment offered nearly a century and a half earlier by Lee, the Cardinal describes "the situation in Haiti" and its relationship to the United States as "a mess" that holds a "horrifying . . . potential for violence." As it did during the Revolution that Toussaint's masters fled, Haiti appears disorderly, chaotic, and violent. And much as he did during his earthly life, Toussaint embodies the opposite of all this. Because he is "a man of peace," the Cardinal "prays for his intercession for the land where he was born into slavery."

O'Connor offers Toussaint as a solution to not just Haiti's current political crisis but also what he perceives as its longstanding dysfunction. According to O'Connor, Haiti is "the land that has known little but oppression, starvation, occupation, terrorism, war, for generation after generation." O'Connor does not identify the specific agents or political forces that have caused these evils, but he does name those who have come to the Haitian people's rescue. According to O'Connor, "the dominant, often the only hope, for the poor [in Haiti] has been by way of their parish churches, their Masses, the efforts of their priests and bishops and, religious sisters and brothers and others."[43] Thus, O'Connor favors Toussaint for not just his ability to intercede on the Haitian people's behalf but also for the way certain aspects of his ministry—namely, his educating poor children and scouring quarantined houses in order to tend to those sick people who had been abandoned—enable him to symbolize the church. Put another way, Toussaint treated forgotten poor of nineteenth-century

43. Cardinal John O'Connor, "In the Cathedral Crypt, a Prayer for Haiti," *Catholic New York*, October 21, 1993, http://tinyurl.com/znx3erz.

New York the same way the Catholic church has treated the poor in Haiti. Because he adapts Toussaint's sainthood for a novel purpose, O'Connor accords it a novel interpretation. Unlike previous hagiographers, O'Connor downplays Toussaint's servile devotion to his mistress as well as his purported opposition to abolitionism and emphasizes his charity for the poor.

But O'Connor's account still shares much in common with previous hagiographical strategies. Through Toussaint, O'Connor crafts a Catholic racial triumphalism updated to fit the needs of his late-twentieth-century context. Thus, when describing what he calls "the situation in Haiti," he recognizes only three actors: one, black Haitians, who have been victimized by anonymous forces; two, the church, which has tirelessly cared for black Haitians; and three, the United States Congress, which did not help to create the problem in Haiti but cannot figure out how to solve it. O'Connor's version of Catholic racial triumphalism shares much in common with other articulations of it: it portrays the church as not just uninvolved in racial evil but resolutely opposed to it; it establishes the church as uniquely capable of saving the lives and securing the happiness of black people; it similarly positions black people as those who receive white people's help as a gift but ought never to agitate for justice on their own. O'Connor's account differs from other forms of Catholic racial triumphalism in two major ways: one, he elevates the church over and against not another religious group but the United States, and two, even though he believes that it cannot help black Haitians as effectively as the church can, O'Connor never doubts that the United States sincerely desires to do so.

Enacting a hagiographical strategy deployed by other champions of the church's racial saints, O'Connor argues that Toussaint provides an example that all people ought to follow, albeit in racially distinct ways. Toussaint represents the church through the way he used his wealth and moral goodness to serve the poor; he serves as a role model for black Haitians due to the way he purportedly rejected what O'Connor condemns as black "militancy" and instead finds freedom inside himself; and in demonstrating the churchly charity to secular politics, Toussaint teaches the United States what it cannot do: save Haiti's black poor. Haiti will enjoy peace only when all three of these actors follow in his example.

Even though O'Connor's Catholic racial triumphalism undoubtedly aims to assert that the church is morally superior to the United States, it also ends up portraying the United States as a morally good force in itself. According to O'Connor, the church wields more power than the United States because politics cannot save Haiti. And, if politics cannot save Haiti, then they likely did not ruin it in the first place. When O'Connor sighs the rhetorical questions, "What has really worked in Haiti? Who really knows what will work now?," he frames "the situation in Haiti" more like an irresolvable math problem than the unsurprising result of centuries of antiblackness, imperialism, and corruption. According to O'Connor's calculus, the United States bears no blame for Haiti's misfortunes; it never sided with white masters or attempted to thwart its revolution; it never occupied Haiti with its military in order to make Haiti's constitution more friendly to American business interests; it never propped up a violent dictator or imposed upon it disastrous economic policies. The United States is only hapless; it has never been guilty.

More than simply historically misinformed, this analysis perpetuates slavery's afterlife. When O'Connor deems political solutions to Haiti's problems not just ineffective but unnecessary, he implies that Haiti has not been wronged. And a country that has not been wronged does not need rights. Perhaps, O'Connor does not believe that a country descended from African slaves can be wronged. Speaking a language that is heavily accented by the afterlife of slavery, O'Connor refrains from using the word *justice* and relies instead on the concepts of "love" and "care." Despite his undoubtedly sincere opposition to the historical practice of chattel slavery, O'Connor still perceives black Haitians as slave-like, albeit unwittingly. Like slaves, Haitians need charity but are not entitled to demand justice.

8.4 Trading Toussaint: Blackness as Ecclesial Commodity

Just as O'Connor used Toussaint in order to promote the ideology of Catholic racial triumphalism, so one of his successors, Cardinal Timothy Dolan, treats blackness as a fungible, hagiographical commodity. In his 2015 homily to mark the start of Black History Month, Dolan contends that, like Moses, Jesus, and Saint Josephine Bakhita, Toussaint "urges us now to embrace the immigrants who arrived today," especially given the fact that they have been "scarred by some nativists within our country."[44] Because he singled out Toussaint and Bakhita, who were both victims of racialized slavery, Dolan initially seemed to respect the uniqueness of antiblackness supremacy. Unfortunately, however, rather than drawing upon their experiences of enslavement in order to express the church's solidarity with black people who continue to endure pervasive antiblackness, Dolan turned their enslaved blackness into a metaphor for the mistreatment that immigrants often experience. In reality, of course, there are black immigrants, but Dolan's homily does not recognize this. Speaking during a mass ostensibly dedicated to Black History Month, Dolan distinguishes blackness from immigrant status when he implies that black people possess a special duty to help immigrants "'pass over' into new life."[45] He in fact encourages black people to spend Black History Month remembering other people's stories and nurturing other people's dreams. Drawing a false analogy between blackness and immigrant status, Dolan turns both blackness and antiblackness into symbols for something else.

Dolan similarly misuses the figure of Moses. Reciting his name alongside those of Toussaint and Bakhita, Dolan at first appears to ascribe to Moses honorary blackness because he led his people out of slavery. But in truth Dolan paradoxically positions Moses as black only so that he can transform him from a fugitive to an immigrant. So Moses becomes fungible the moment he is imagined as metaphorically black.

44. Beth Griffin, "Black History Month Opens with Mass at St. Patrick's Cathedral," *National Catholic Reporter*, February 3, 2015, http://tinyurl.com/hjqqnl3.
45. Ibid.

Rather than respecting the role that Moses has played in black Catholic history, Dolan exploits it. Moses becomes fungible the moment he is imagined as metaphorically black. Although some black people have arrived in the United States through immigration, they represent an except and not the rule, especially in the collective imagination. Dolan's homily recognizes that black people typically are incorporated into the United States not as descendants of immigrants but as slaves. Dolan has erased black Catholics from their own story.

8.5 Unimaginable Fugitivity: The Haitian Revolution and Hagiographical Denial

The Revolution that Toussaint's master fled tells a story that many white Catholics still do not want to hear. In Haiti, black slaves fled and sometimes killed their masters. They did not love them. They did not wish to continue living for them any longer. These black fugitives did not need white saviors: they overthrew their masters and turned back Napoleon's forces almost entirely on their own. Even the few Polish soldiers who deserted and joined the black revolutionaries would be considered legally black the moment they acquired Haitian citizenship.[46]

Like nineteenth-century, slave-owning, U.S.-American whites, contemporary white Catholics still fear the Haitian Revolution. It also seems nearly unimaginable: white Catholics cannot believe that black people achieved their own freedom. But as demonstrated by its interpretation of Toussaint's holiness, the church also seeks to anathematize it. Just as "the Western world . . . considers [the Haitian Revolution and] society" as secular "heresies," so white Catholics similarly classify them as theologically heretical.[47] The church's

46. Nina Glick Schiller and Georges Eugene Fouron, "'The Blood Remains Haitian': Race, Nation, and Belonging in the Transmigrant Experience," in Philip W. Scher, *Perspectives on the Caribbean: A Reader in Culture, History, and Representation* (West Sussex, UK: John Wiley & Sons, 2010), 261.

47. Neil Roberts, *Freedom as Marronage: The Dialectic of Slavery and Freedom: Arendt, Pettit, Rousseau, Douglass, and the Haitian Revolution* (PhD diss., The University of Chicago, 2007), 180. For more on the "heretical" character of black radical philosophy and intellectual thought, see Anthony Bogues, *Black Heretics, Black Prophets: Radical Political Intellectuals* (New York: Routledge, 2003), 12–16.

collective antipathy toward the Haitian Revolution does not result from its disapproval of violent revolution itself: many American nations, including the United States, gained independence due only to war. Yet the church's hagiographical processes condemn only one of them: Haiti's.[48] Nor can we attribute this displeasure to longstanding Catholic respect for political authority. Even in the thirteenth century, Thomas Aquinas recognized that human beings possessed a duty to obey only legitimate authorities: he explicitly identified a tyrant as lacking legitimacy. For this reason, a tyrant could be deposed or even killed.[49] Only antiblackness supremacy made white mastery over black slaves appear non-tyrannical and therefore legitimate.[50] Toussaint's ecclesial afterlife suggests that contemporary Catholics still struggle to perceive slave resistance as holy.

Partially because the church cannot grasp black fugitivity as holy, it cannot recognize white mastership as truly evil. Consider a final aspect of Cardinal O'Connor's 1993 defense of Toussaint. Preempting those who would ask whether Toussaint was "an Uncle Tom to be scorned by those who believed he should have been a militant against slavery," O'Connor contended, "If ever a man was truly free, it was Pierre Toussaint." According to O'Connor, Toussaint in fact "felt so free interiorly that he seemed indifferent to his own state of technical bondage."[51] Like other hagiographers of racial saints, O'Connor dramatized the racism Toussaint endured in order to ultimately trivialize it.[52] O'Connor also misrepresents the history of the church as

48. In fact, some Americans who have been placed on the path to sainthood explicitly endorsed and sometimes participated in their country's independence movements. See for example Venerable Félis Varela of Cuba. For an overview of U.S. Americans who have been canonized and beatified, see http://www.usccb.org/prayer-and-worship/prayers-and-devotions/saints/american-saints-and-blesseds.cfm. Accessed December 20, 2016.
49. Anna Floerke Scheid, *Just Revolution: A Christian Ethic of Political Resistance and Social Transformation* (Lanham, MD: Lexington, 2015), 26.
50. For more on the history of Catholic thinking about revolution, see Scheid, *Just Revolution*, 71–108.
51. O'Connor, "In the Cathedral Crypt."
52. O'Connor somewhat strangely insists that "legions of slaves purchased their freedom from this man." I tried to find evidence that Toussaint freed anyone but his wife and sister but could not find any. Regardless of the historical data, O'Connor misleads the audience when he implies that Toussaint had the power to free other slaves. In societies in which slavery is legal, only slave masters can free their slaves. Even if Toussaint gave many other black people the money required to buy their own freedom, it would be inaccurate to say that these other slaves "purchased their freedom from" Toussaint.

well as Toussaint's sainthood. According to O'Connor, the church has celebrated Toussaint's "indifference" to his enslavement only because it loves freedom so much. Echoing the arguments of earlier Catholic apologists, O'Connor submits the church's support for black slavery as evidence of its opposition to it.

Like other Catholics who perceived slavery as a form of freedom, O'Connor ultimately contradicts himself. If "true freedom" emerges only when one learns to be "indifferent to his own state of technical bondage" as O'Connor claimed, then only black people can be free. After all, if one can find "true freedom" only by learning to adopt the proper attitude to one's enslavement, then should not everyone seek to become a slave? O'Connor of course does not believe this. Like many other white Catholics, O'Connor counseled actual slavery as the path to true freedom for blacks only. How can the church hate either Africanized slavery or its afterlife until it learns to love those who have refused to be slaves?

9

———

Toward a Fugitive Hagiography

The sainthoods of Claver, Porres, and Toussaint prove that, although the overwhelming majority of contemporary U.S. Catholics oppose the actual practice of slavery, both individual white Catholics and the church as a corporate body still struggle to shed their hagiographical attachment to black servility. This tendency has taken hold of the church's corporate body as a bad habit. The hagiographical renown of these three men animates slavery's afterlife due not only to the errors of misguided individuals only but also to the way they adhere to standardized scripts of Catholic holiness. As occurred in the case of Sister Preher, for example, the stories themselves can even override the good intentions and right political reason of Catholic whites.

As a corporate vice, antiblackness supremacy will not accede to mere moral suasion; the church can banish its bad racial habits only by building new ones. Moral suasion does have a role to play, however: the church must learn to think differently as it learns to act differently. Both aspects of habit building intensify the other: acting differently makes thinking differently easier and vice versa. But although the church can acquire new racial habits only if it chooses to do so, it cannot do so entirely on its own.[1] For this reason, the church must be acted upon as much as it acts; it must experience that which it hates in order to love in the way that it ought. The church cannot relinquish its affinity for white mastership by seeking to become its own master.

Since the church both participates in the secular afterlife of slavery and perpetuates its own, it can be racially re-habituated only through sustained encounter with black fugitivity understood as both a historical practice and a principle of hagiographical interpretation. As a principle of hagiographical interpretation, black fugitivity both re-orients the church's hagiographical imagination and corrects the church's perception of its own racial virtue. It also clarifies the path forward: only black fugitivity dismantles slavery's afterlife unequivocally. The church ought to choose to support and empower black fugitivity when it can, but it will also need to suffer black fugitivity when it cannot. Rather than perceiving itself as a body that protects black people, the church must recognize itself as a space from which black people often have needed to flee. Rather than considering itself an agent that gives black people love, the church must accept itself as a structure from which black people often have needed to take justice. Black fugitivity ultimately compels the church to relinquish its hold on captive persons and memories.

Like slavery, fugitivity can be misunderstood.[2] During the era of legalized slavery, fugitivity encompassed any attempt to escape a master's custody and/or flee his property. But black fugitivity comprises more than the act of physical flight; it also includes occasions in which enslaved black people moved themselves to spaces that were inaccessible to white supervision and/or unsanctioned by white power. This owes to the nature of the slave master's power: she dominates her property by placing them in strategic proximity to her. Since the afterlife of slavery strives to sustain, if not the actual practice of slavery, then the stigmatizing association between blackness and slave status, black people have continued to enact fugitivity up until the present day. The legally mandated segregation that characterizes

---

1. Thomas Aquinas, *Summa Theologica*, Ia–IIae. 49, 2 ad 3; 55, 4 ad 6.
2. My definition of fugitivity overlaps significantly with but is not identical to Roberts' use of the term "marronage" (*Freedom As Marronage: The Dialectic*, 9–11).

Jim Crow only appears a sharp break from the racially integrated plantation society it replaced. Even then, white people attempted to control the ways black people occupied space; white Southerners did not simply insist on the whites-only water fountain and lunch counter, they also held on to black people as sharecroppers and domestics. As during the era of legalized slavery, black people who fled Jim Crow's systemic captivity were tortured and killed.[3] For these reasons, the Great Migration and the Civil Rights Movement qualify as acts of black fugitivity.[4] Both movements dealt death blows to Jim Crow because in both cases black people refused to remain in place. During the Great Migration, black people fled white people's disciplining violence; during the Civil Rights Movement, black people used this violence to expose white supremacy as evil.

So Northern patterns of antiblackness supremacy similarly strive to dictate where black people can live and how they ought to comport themselves in public places. Non-black people inflict the structural violence of segregated schools and disproportionately black prisons and the direct interpersonal violence of extrajudicial executions on black people for the same reason: they perceive black spatial liberty as inherently threatening.[5] When a non-black Latino police officer in Minnesota shoots a black passenger for complying with his commands, he does so out of not hate but fear.[6] He believes that the seated and calmly speaking black passenger will harm him as long as he remains un-subjugated. It is fear of black freedom that keeps black people in chains. For this reason, black fugitivity takes many shapes, including but not limited to the following: when a black person enters the wrong neighborhood at the wrong time of day; when black people claim spaces as their own and attempt to exclude nonblack people from

3. Angela Y. Davis, *Abolition Democracy: Beyond Prison, Torture, and Empire* (New York: Seven Stories, 2005), 53–54; Cameron McWhirter, *Red Summer: The Summer of 1919 and the Awakening of Black America* (New York: Henry Holt and Company, 2011).
4. Roberts, *Freedom as Marronage*, 202.
5. Davis, *Abolition Democracy*, 35, 37.
6. Sharon LaFraniere and Mitch Smith, "Philando Castile Was Pulled Over 49 Times in 13 Years, Often for Minor Infractions." *The New York Times,* July 16, 2016. http://www.nytimes.com/2016/07/17/us/before-philando-castiles-fatal-encounter-a-costly-trail-of-minor-traffic-stops.html. Accessed July 26, 2016.

joining them; or when black people refuse to submit or appear to refuse to submit to surveillance by nonblack civilians or by police officers or other state agents of any color.[7]

9.1 Fugitivity as a Diagnostic Tool

The first way black fugitivity can help the church build new racial habits is by forcing it to select slavery and its ongoing afterlife as our frame of analysis: after all, there can be fugitives only if there are slave masters. In thrusting slavery into the spotlight, black fugitivity also forces us to examine it thoroughly. Rather than a generalized form of oppression or a metaphor for evil, slavery operates as a distinct relation of power. It differs from other forms of injustice at least as much as it resembles them. One insight leads to another: slavery's afterlife also qualifies as unique.

Black fugitivity diagnoses the church's hagiographical imagination as flawed in a second way. As demonstrated in their esteem for white men such as Claver, Slattery, La Farge, and Markoe, white Catholics typically perceive white people's affection for black people as virtuous or inherently anti-racist. But in illuminating the link between antiblackness supremacy and the afterlife of slavery, black fugitivity enables us to appreciate the ambivalence of white desires for both blackness and black people. Just as a mistress strives to keep her slave at bay in some circumstances and to hold her close in others, so have white people still maintained a paradoxical relation to both blackness and black people. In truth, white people have not simply segregated themselves from black people; they also often attempt to curate strategic proximity with black people. White people do not necessarily hate black people; they often desire them intensely. American popular music and culture testify to the strength of white people's desire for both blackness and black people.

Third, in redefining the problem, black fugitivity also reimagines the solution. When we uphold Jim Crow–style segregation as the

---

7. Roberts, *Freedom as Marronage*, 202, 213; Robin D.G. Kelley, *Freedom Dreams: The Black Radical Imagination* (Boston: Beacon, 2002), 16–17.

unchanging essence of antiblack racism, white aspirations for racial proximity are easily misinterpreted as evidence of racial progress. When we locate the essence of racial evil in hatefulness, bigotry, or segregation, we similarly overestimate the corrective power of love, tolerance, and proximity. But fugitivity discredits these assessments. It reminds us that white people perpetuate racial evil neither by hating black people nor by seeking distance from them but by maintaining masterly power to hold black people in place. The church cannot oppose antiblackness supremacy unless it attempts to strip white people of this power.

Fugitivity both contributes to the church's corporate rehabituation and serves as a measure of it in a fourth way. Vicious habits do more than simply distort our understanding of the world; they also implant perverse desires within us. The former reinforces the latter and vice versa: we believe what we want to believe, and what we believe justifies what we desire. Exposure to black fugitivity proves to the church that it hates black fugitivity. It will be difficult if not impossible for the church to empower a reality that it wishes would disappear. The church's affective response to black fugitivity also provides a marker of the church's moral progress. Like all moral agents, the church will not qualify as virtuous simply by acquiring the ability to perform morally good acts for the right reasons; true virtue exists only when one derives pleasure from the exercise of virtue. Rightly ordered pleasure also sustains virtue: no mere rubber stamp on a moral project that has already been completed, pleasure enhances our capacity to achieve moral goodness.[8] In order to fully align its corporate body against antiblackness supremacy, the church must acquire the capacity to embrace black fugitivity rather than fear it.

9.2 Fugitivity as a Historical Practice

Black fugitivity unsettles the afterlife of slavery in both the world and the church as not just a diagnostic tool but also as a historical

---

8. Thomas Aquinas, *Summa Theologica* IIa–IIae 59, 2 ad 2.

practice. It does so not simply because it ends enslavement but how it does so. By exiting, the fugitive ripped a hole in the slave master's cosmology. More than simply disobeying her master, a fugitive left him. Overturning the ideology that portrayed the slave as grateful just to be alive, the fugitive proved that she would rather die than continue living in sometimes intimate proximity to her master. She refused to live not just *for* her master but also *with* him. The farther away a slave strayed from her master, the less control her master wielded over her. Like all parasites, slave masters sustained their own lives by feeding off the bodies of their enslaved prey. Fugitivity therefore threatened to deprive slave masters not just of their way of life but of life itself.

Fugitivity interrupts slavery's afterlife even more than other anti-slavery strategies such as abolition or emancipation.[9] Toussaint's hagiographical afterlife in particular demonstrates why. Toussaint attained freedom not through his own will but his mistress's: it was a gift he was given rather than a debt he was owed. Crediting his life and freedom to her largesse, he remained indebted to her all the days of his life. Because it portrays even freedom as a gift a slave receives from her merciful master, emancipation can flatter a slave master's ego.[10] For this same reason, it ultimately fails to correct slavery's central mistake: a slave master harms his slave not by declining to treat her with sufficient kindness but by refusing to grant her justice. Manumission gives freedom as a gift when it is owed as a right.[11]

Despite the fact that abolition typically frees enslaved people against their masters' wills, it too can uphold slavery's afterlife. Abolition differs from emancipation primarily in that it positions not the master but the state as enslaved people's liberating benefactor. For example, citing the sacrifice their Union Army ancestors made in purportedly fighting for black people's freedom, many white people still attempt to undermine their black countrywomen and -men's demands for justice.[12] According to these whites, any debt white people may have

---

9. Stephen Best and Saidiya Hartman, "Fugitive Justice," *Representations* 92, no. 1 (Fall 2005): 2–3.
10. Patterson, *Slavery and Social Death*, 224, 241.
11. Farley, "Apogee of the Commodity," 1237.
12. Jonathan Chait, "Why Limbaugh Can't Stop Talking about Slavery," *New York*, October 6, 2014,

owed black people has already been paid off. This trope contains a further implication: in addition to ceasing their demands for justice, black people should express gratitude to white saviors. While white men were allowed to pick up arms purportedly to liberate blacks, black people are not allowed to use violence in order to liberate themselves.

But fugitivity alone shatters racialized slavery's central logic. Fugitivity seizes freedom as a though it were a right. A fugitive escapes her captors; she does not thank them.[13] More than simply stripping a former captor of the power to act as a mistress, fugitivity denies her the chance to identify as a liberator. And in contrast to manumission and emancipation, which can encourage the former slave to remain close to her liberator, fugitivity places the former slave out of reach. While manumission, emancipation, and abolition undoubtedly end enslavement, only fugitivity truly interrupts its afterlife.

9.3 Racial Sainthood as an Enemy of Black Fugitivity

Largely due to the way in which it undermines both slavery and its afterlife, the racial sainthoods of Claver, Porres, and Toussaint have opposed black fugitivity even more than they have supported the actual practice of slavery. Claver, for example, reconciled slaves to their masters; he punished fugitivity as a sin; he policed the consciences of black slaves in the confessional; and he helped the city of Cartagena complete its victory over the black fugitives of the Limón Palenque. Brought in to hear these condemned men confess that their fugitivity had been a sin, Claver turned the sacrament of confession into an instrument of slave-catching.[14] Slavery presented a captive with a choice: be a slave or die. One could be free and dead or enslaved and alive; one could not be both. For this reason, a slave master could

http://tinyurl.com/zlkn2h2; Allen C. Guelzo, "Should Blacks Get Reparations?," *Christian Science Monitor*, July 16, 2009, http://tinyurl.com/homd5nv.

13. Moten, "Case of Blackness," 179.

14. Kathryn Joy McKnight, "Elder, Slave and Solider: Maroon Voices from the Palenque del Limón, 1634," in *Afro-Latino Voices*, ed. Kathryn Joy McKnight and Leo J. Garofalo (Indianapolis: Hackett Publishing Company, 2009), 64–70; Splendiani, *Proceso*, 310; Arana, "Pedro Claver y la evangelizacion en Cartagena," 312; United States Conference of Catholic Bishops, "The Corporal Works of Mercy," USCCB.org, New Evangelization, accessed July 28, 2016, http://tinyurl.com/jry25xf.

portray his violence as a merciful gift. Thus, when Claver instructed condemned *palenqueros* that they must confess their sins of fugitivity and rebellion or suffer eternal damnation, he imposed on them that same choice between enslaved life and liberated death. And in absolving them of these so-called sins, Claver acted mercifully toward them only to the extent that we believe those men deserved both the social death of slavery and the eternal death of damnation. After Cartagena's civil authorities successfully recaptured the *palenqueros's* menacingly fugitive bodies, he set about to recapture their fugitive souls.

As previously demonstrated, Porres and Toussaint also discouraged black fugitivity during their earthly lives. Porres portrayed black submission to white disciplinary violence as holy; he also tamed black slaves, turning them from while animals and enemies into harmless but useful pets. So Toussaint condemned all forms of fugitivity, especially those displayed by black Haitians, declaring them unholy, unwise, harmful, and essentially violent. All three men treated black fugitivity as the enemy of peace and social order.

Their saintly afterlives have similarly opposed black fugitivity during the afterlife of slavery. In the United States, abolition has wreaked particular havoc on the church's hagiographical imagination. Habituated by residence in a society that portrayed black freedom as a gift of the state, white Catholic racial reformers perceived freedom as somehow extrinsic to black people. Similarly habituated by membership in a church that had long doubted the authenticity of black freedom, white Catholic racial reformers could imagine freedom as a gift that only they and their church could truly secure for black people. As the missionaries of this church, they positioned themselves as great emancipators: like innocent but heroic bystanders, they purported to liberate black people from captivity at the hands of a third party. They believed that they intervened in racial oppression but shared no guilt in it. Catholic racial vices intermingled with U.S.-American ones.

Although these activists genuinely desired that black people attain equal rights, they preferred that black people received them either from whites or because of them. For this reason, these alleged protectors and defenders of black people used their power to make black fugitivity more difficult. After all, if black people were fugitives, then white people could not be liberators. White Catholics desired black gratitude more than black freedom. They believed that black people would find happiness if they only knew their place—in the church in particular and society in general. They attempted to save black people by convincing them that they ought to be grateful to both the church and its white priests. While fugitivity recognizes the wisdom of impatience and self-reliance, these white Catholics counseled black people to wait patiently for whites to do the right thing.

9.4 Fugitivity as a Principle of Hagiographical Re-Interpretation

Fugitivity re-habituates the church not simply by allowing the church to define antiblackness supremacy more accurately and depriving white people of masterly power and its attendant pleasures.[15] Because the church also sustains the ecclesial afterlife of slavery by the way it makes memories, especially of itself, its rehabituation requires fugitive memories as well as people. In this way, black fugitivity understood as a principle of hagiographical interpretation unsettles the ecclesial afterlife of slavery just as surely as historical acts of fugitivity undermined the institution of slavery.[16] Like fugitives from Cartagena, Lima, and San Domingue, fugitive memories threaten the survival of worlds they have escaped precisely by their refusal to live inside of them.[17]

This fugitive approach to hagiography first requires that the church learn to appreciate the holiness of its black fugitives, both those who

---

15. Farley, "Apogee of the Commodity," 1235.
16. This resembles what Roberts describes as Martinican writer Édouard Glissant's concept of "intellectual marronage" (*Freedom as Marronage*, 14).
17. Frank B. Wilderson III, *Red, White & Black: Cinema and the Structure of U.S. Antagonisms* (Durham, NC: Duke University Press, 2010), 58; Fred Moten, "Blackness and Nothingness (Mysticism in the Flesh)," *South Atlantic Quarterly* 112, no. 4 (2013): 737–80, at 739.

have evaded capture by the church's processes of hagiographical memory-making as well as those who left the church itself. The church's hagiographical fugitives there include not just African-born Muslims, atheists, and animists but also all black people who sought to create a communal relationship with Christ outside the space of slavery. In fleeing the church, the church's fugitives did not necessarily flee relationship with Christ. For example, some members of a seventeenth-century Colombian *palenque* called Limon "lived in Christianity, knew the prayers, sustained the church, and prayed the rosary" in a space outside of Spanish captivity.[18] Those who enacted fugitivity from the institutional church un-coincidentally qualify as hagiographical fugitives as well: the church's hagiographical imagination simply could not grasp the memory of those who existed in spaces beyond the reach of white mastership.

The church also ought to appreciate the moral goodness of those fugitives who rejected not just the church but Christ as well. Why? A belief that black people were better off as Christianized slaves of white masters than they were as unbaptized free women and men helps to cement the church's hagiographical alliance with antiblackness supremacy. Like other apologies for the church's participating in Europe's colonizing projects, this thinking portrays the church's missionaries as flawed but ultimately well-intentioned individuals. Even if they deployed unjust means, they pursued evangelization as an undeniably good end. All of these claims imply that it is better to be brought inside the church than to be allowed to remain outside it.

But this too closely resembles that particularly repugnant trope of secular antiblackness, which expects African Americans to be grateful that they were born in America rather than Africa. Even worse, this rhetorical move inevitably implies that black people ought to be thankful for slavery as well.[19] So the church's perceptions of its own missionary past often establish a similar discursive dynamic: slavery

18. Jane Landers, "Founding Mothers: Female Rebels in Colonial New Granada and Spanish Florida," *Journal of African American History* 98, no. 1 (2013): 8–9.
19. D. Wreck, "Pat Buchanan: Slavery Best Thing Ever to Happen to Blacks," *Daily Kos*, March 22, 2008, http://tinyurl.com/zcb9uk3.

seemed like a more-than-fair price to pay to be spared the eternal death one deserved as a sinner. White Catholics, in contrast, were believed to have been ransomed through infant baptism. They inherited their salvation from a long line of purportedly Catholic ancestors. Africans, instead, were snatched from eternal death by slave catchers. While black people should, of course, be permitted to express gratitude for the historical circumstances that have shaped their lives, they should not be expected to feel this way.

The early-twentieth-century black Catholic educator Constance Daniel models black fugitivity from the church. Constance joined the Catholic Church as a fugitive from the Unitarian Church, which she perceived as pervasively racist. She soon discovered that the Catholic Church provided no safe haven: the racism that drove her from one church was waiting for her at the next. In 1924, the founders of the newly opened Cardinal Gibbon Institute appointed her husband as its principal and her as its assistant principal.[20] Wanting to provide their students what theologian Cecilia Moore terms "an emancipatory education" aimed at transmitting "knowledge of [black] history and culture," this husband-and-wife team soon clashed with the school's predominantly white board of trustees, which preferred to limit the curriculum to so-called industrial training.[21]

Unsurprisingly, the board's policy intended to pacify both Daniels and her black pupils. In a letter to the school's director, Archbishop Michael J. Curley, one of these white power brokers decried the Daniels' "idea of raising the Negro race to a higher plane." Although he believed it to be "of course is well enough in its own way . . . [it] was not exactly the idea the institution started out with, nor would it be suited to this section of the country at this time."[22] The Daniels, in contrast, intended the exact opposite of this. They promoted education as a form of black emancipation from the aftereffects of slavery.[23]

20. Cecilia A. Moore, "Victor and Constance Daniel and Emancipatory Education at the Cardinal Gibbons Institute," *Journal of Catholic Education* 4, no. 3 (2001): 397.
21. Ibid., 398.
22. Ibid.
23. Ibid., 401.

They recognized that even the most well-intentioned whites remained habituated by slavery: as Moore explains, these whites believed that "African Americans were to be helped, to be saved, to be taken care of, and to be controlled, but not to be accorded respect."[24]

Due partially but not entirely to her encounter with such white paternalism, Daniel considered church membership increasingly unbearable. In a letter to the institute's cofounder La Farge, Daniel decried the church as pervasively racist. After declaring both her antipathy toward white priests and her abandonment of the sacrament of confession, she plainly stated, "If race and creed clash, creed will have to go. I am a Negro first."[25] But La Farge rejected her account as inaccurate. Unable to acknowledge that the church expressed habits of racialized slave mastership, La Farge could not understand how anyone would ever leave it. Insisting that "the Catholic Church from her intrinsic holiness infallibly renders justice in the end," La Farge maintained that the solutions to the country's racial problems were always found within the church and never outside it. For this reason, he "chastised Daniel for her lack of faith in the church" and "urged [her to] prudence [and] patience."[26] He exhorted her to "nonaggressive," "dispassionate," "gradual," "moderate," and "conciliatory." As if putting her emancipatory pedagogical philosophy into practice, Daniel refused to be pacified: she believed that "blacks could not afford to wait for the white Catholic hierarchy" to act on their behalf.[27]

Daniel embodied holy fugitivity from a Catholic Church voluntarily aligned with antiblackness supremacy. She refused to follow racialized scripts of black femininity; she rebuked the authority of paternalistic whites. She pursued black self-emancipation as an end in itself. She was willing to flee the Catholic Church if it continued to hold her captive. Although the church should remember her, it should not try to recapture her; it instead ought to make itself a body that Daniel never would have desired to flee. Although the church ought to learn how

24. Ibid., 400.
25. Southern, *John La Farge*, 41.
26. Ibid.
27. Ibid., 42.

to acknowledge fugitivity as a form of holiness, it should not elevate its fugitives to sainthood—at least not in the foreseeable future. First, for the most part, the church cannot remember these women and men; their histories, like their holiness, has been lost not just to the church but to historians as well. This elusiveness in fact supplies fugitivity with much of its re-habituating power. Second, even if the church could locate its fugitives amid historical records, it should not seek to capture them. The church should instead train itself to remember that it has not remembered them. Why? In turning its fugitives into saintly expressions of itself, the church forgets itself. In truth, the church did not seek to create a space outside of slaveocracy; it felt perfectly at home inside it. It did not facilitate black fugitivity as much as it helped to make it necessary. Third, canonizing these fugitives would paradoxically recapture them. Rather than allowing itself to be interrupted by the dangerous memories that come to the church from a fugitive outside, the church seeks to capture this fugitive past and claim it as its own.[28]

The church's hagiographical memories have enslaved not just black people, but the concept of blackness.[29] As demonstrated by the hagiographical afterlives of Porres and Toussaint, the church has treated blackness as a fungible hagiograhical commodity. In so doing, it has upheld slavery's afterlife. Why? Just as slavery allowed white masters to turn black people in to nearly any product and compel them to perform nearly any task, so the afterlife of slavery has deployed blackness as "the imaginative surface upon which the master and the nation came to understand themselves."[30] From the wildly popular mid-nineteenth-century phenomenon of blackface minstrelsy to twenty-first-century pop culture, "the black body [serves] . . . as the vehicle of white self-exploration, renunciation, and enjoyment."[31] Still today, nonblack people make blackness whatever they need it to be.[32]

28. Moten, "Case of Blackness," 179.
29. For more on this, see Moten, "Case of Blackness," 187–88; Wilderson, *Red, White, and Black*, 58.
30. Hartman, *Scenes of Subjection*, 8.
31. Ibid., 26. See also Eric Lott, *Love and Theft: Blackface Minstrelsy and the American Working Class* (New York: Oxford University Press, 1993).
32. Wilderson, *Red, White, and Black*, 21, 58–59.

This tendency to appropriate blackness extends beyond the cultural sphere. Nonblack people of color, including nonblack women, workers, and LGBT people, all analogize their struggles either to the fight against slavery or to the fight for black civil rights. But this rhetorical tactic does not build upon black movements for freedom; it delegitimizes them. Like those contemporary nonblack U.S. Americans who put on blackness in order to position themselves as rebellious, hypermasculine, or cool, these political groups proclaim themselves not just the "new" blacks but the "real" blacks. In superseding black people in this way, these groups share "refuse to admit to significant differences of structural position born of discrepant histories between blacks and their political allies, actual or potential."[33] Unfortunately, as demonstrated by the hagiographical afterlives of Porres and Toussaint, black fungibility also has provided the church a means of self-affirmation and creation. And in downplaying or implicitly denying the uniqueness of antiblackness supremacy, the church does not simply misrepresent the truth; it animates slavery's afterlife. We must no longer treat blackness as an entity that can be exchanged for or turned into whatever we desire. Black people are not an analogy; they are not like money, which both measures the value of other goods and can be turned into them.

9.5 Remembering Fugitives and Not Just Victims

In its focus on the re-habituating power of memory, this project undoubtedly takes inspiration from the German-born, twentieth-century theologian Johann Baptist Metz. Writing in the aftermath of World War Two and the Holocaust, he searched for theological meaning in the largescale suffering and death these events wrought. Rather than attempting to explain how God could allow such evil, Metz eventually realized that the crucified Christ stands in solidarity with all of history's victims. The church ought to therefore remember these victims and tell their stories publicly as a way of uncovering

33. Jared Sexton, "People-of-Color-Blindness: Notes on the Afterlife of Slavery," *Social Text* 28, no. 2 (June 20, 2010): 47–48.

discrete histories as not innocent but marred by evil. Metz believed that keeping history's victims alive in this way would endanger the ideologies that justified current evils.

This project undoubtedly shares Metz's hope that memory can be dangerous, but it also disagrees with him. In the case of antiblackness supremacy, the church ought to remember not just its victims as Metz's proposes but also its fugitives. The church's fugitive memories in fact preserve the church's ability to remember its black victims in a way that runs against the grain of antiblackness supremacy. Although Metz conceded the church's status as *semper reformanda*, his desire to rouse the church to prophetic action against the world perhaps led him to underestimate the extent to which the church had helped to construct the very histories he wished to interrupt.[34] In other words, Metz focused primarily on the church as a body that remembers rather than a body that must also remember itself.

Metz also underestimated the extent to which a community can use the memory of its past victims in order to draw attention away from the ways in which it continues to victimize these people in the present. For example, rather than illuminating continuities between past and present, in the contemporary United States, stories about the historical mistreatment of black people more often serve to portray racial justice as a fait accompli. We condemn the racial past as a rhetorical tactic: the United States is not that bad since it is not as bad as it was. My project differs from Metz's in a further way: while Metz's call to remember history's victims risks reducing black people to what they suffered, recollecting the church's fugitives highlights the intensity of their resistance.[35] The church's fugitives are more than victims of antiblackness supremacy; they loom as its mortal enemy. History's victims endanger social injustice because they were defeated. The church's fugitives endanger antiblackness supremacy, however, because they triumphed over it.[36]

Black fugitivity also helps the church follow Metz's prescription that

---

34. Ekkehard Schuster and Reinhold Boschert-Kimmig, *Hope against Hope: Johann Baptist Metz and Elie Wiesel Speak Out on the Holocaust*, trans. J. Matthew Ashley (New York: Paulist Press, 1999), 38.
35. For a good overview of these critiques, see McLean, "'Do This in Memory of Me,'" 296–301.

it exist as "an exodus community and an eschatological community."[37] More than simply reminding the church of the ways in which it has acted as the enemy of exodus, the memory of black fugitivity provides a historical example of how to enact it. In so doing, it helps to fine-tune the church's eschatological imagination, making the church neither nostalgic for the past nor self-satisfied about the present. Because it is an inherently unsettled state, fugitivity can orient the church to the eschaton by reminding us of the incompleteness of our redemption. As long as slave masters scour the countryside, a fugitive remains only incompletely and provisionally free. Fugitivity prevents the church from mistaking racial justice as finished business.[38] As Jared Sexton reminds us, "Fugitivity is not freedom, or [at least] not yet."[39] Reminding the church of what it could not apprehend, fugitivity proves not only that the past was different than we remember it but also that it could have been different than it was. In so doing, fugitivity unveils the future as similarly elusive.

9.5 Proposals for Hagiographical Strategies That Facilitate Fugitivity

In light of black fugitivity's antagonism to the church's bad racial habits, the church ought to implement the following hagiographical strategies. First, it ought to abandon the search for white heroes, at least for the foreseeable future. While some white Catholics certainly have embodied racial virtue, the church currently lacks the capacity to recognize them in a way that does not reaffirm vicious racial ideologies. Second, the church also ought to cease praising those white Catholics who have already been exalted as racial heroes, such as Claver, La Farge, and Slattery. In celebrating white people such as Slattery and La Farge for their purported racial righteousness, the

36. Édouard Glissant, *Caribbean Discourse: Selected Essays* (Charlottesville: University Press of Virginia, 1989), 248.
37. Johann Baptist Metz, *Theology of the World*, trans. William Glen-Doepel (New York: Seabury, 1969), 93–94 as found in McLean, "Do This in Memory of Me," 25.
38. Moten, "Case of Blackness," 202.
39. Jared Sexton, "Afro-pessimism."

church further establishes whiteness as a measuring stick of morality. These men appear racially virtuous only by comparison with other even less racially virtuous whites. Would they not seem morally ordinary at best if compared with black Catholics? Their purported racial virtue also portrays racial justice as a gift that valiant white folks bestow upon black people rather than a debt they owe them. When one repays a debt, she merely wipes the slate clean; she only returns what she has taken. We should not make saints out of those who partially repair a world they have helped to break.

Men such as Slattery, Markoe, and La Farge are remembered in large part because they belonged to large religious orders: their memories are automatically preserved by a tightly knit and well-organized body. In promoting the holiness of Claver the Jesuit and Porres the Dominican, they narrated an autobiography of not just the church but the specific religious order to which they belonged. Unfortunately, however, the church has perpetuated antiblackness supremacy not despite the existence of these orders but partially because of them. Also, because black Catholics were systematically denied ordination and shut out of religious life, they have been unable to access some of the church's most reliable channels of memory. As it has the sacraments of Baptism, the Eucharist, and Matrimony, antiblackness supremacy has enlisted another of the church's most sacred structures in its service. Rather than seeking to vindicate the order by searching for racial heroes, Catholic religious communities may need to reckon with the fact that their communities either did not produce or could not recognize authentic examples of racial virtue.

Fugitivity prescribes a third strategy for memory. When contemporary Catholics wish to invoke the memory of Catholic racial righteousness, they instead should call upon black Catholics like Thomas Wyatt Turner, Daniel A. Rudd, Fr. August Thompson, and Dr. Arthur Falls, among many underappreciated others.[40] But they cannot do so uncritically; although she does not adopt the fugitive

40. LaReine-Marie Mosely, "Daniel A. Rudd and His *American Catholic Tribune*: Faithful and Prophetic in Passing On the Tradition," in *Uncommon Faithfulness: The Black Catholic Experience*, ed. M. Shawn Copeland (Maryknoll, NY: Orbis, 2009); Katrina M. Sanders, "Black Catholic Clergy and the

hagiography proposed in this book, M. Shawn Copeland models hagiographical strategies that complement it. In her theological biography of servant of God Henriette Delille, the free woman of color who helped to found the Sisters of the Holy Family in New Orleans, Copeland resists the temptation to retroactively place the church, whether conceived of as an institution or a corporate body, on the side of racial justice.[41] Delille sometimes fought against the church's corporate body rather than simply working within it.[42] In addition to illuminating the possibilities of black resistance to ecclesial injustice, Copeland also points out its limitations.[43] Even as we admire Delille's creativity, courage, and obedience to God's call, Copeland instills in us a heavy sorrow for the harm that white supremacy and patriarchy caused her. In contrast, hagiographies of Claver, Porres, and Toussaint may occasion the reader to pity enslaved black people, but they do not encourage the reader to either lament or feel angry about the long history of slavery.[44] They expose the rough edges of history only so that they can smooth them away.

Precisely because we cannot describe Delille's holiness without indicting the church of racial evil, her life story unsettles us; it testifies to the "already but not yet" of our redemption. A comparison with Claver's sainthood again proves instructive. While Claver's sainthood has been used to portray the church as a body that brings salvation to black people, Delille's sainthood teaches the church that it needs to be saved from its sinful antiblackness. If interpreted correctly, Delille's life story can remind the church that the saints ultimately exist to point out not just what God has done in history but also what God will

Struggle for Civil Rights," in Copeland, *Uncommon Faithfulness*; Rice, "Confronting the Heresy," 59–77.

41. Copeland, *Subversive Power of Love*, 5, 7–8, 17–19, 44–46.

42. Ibid., 66.

43. For more on the way "the real-lived texture of Black life requires moral agency that may run contrary to the ethical boundaries of mainline [religion]" and how "blacks may use action guides that have never been considered within the scope of traditional codes of faithful living," see Katie Geneva Cannon, *Katie's Canon: Womanism and the Soul of the Black Community* (London: Bloomsbury Academic, 1998), 58.

44. For more on the role that lamentation plays in the pursuit of racial justice, see Bryan N. Massingale, *Racial Justice and the Catholic Church* (Maryknoll, NY: Orbis, 2010), 104–15.

do. More than simply paving new roads of holiness, the saints should also tell us how far we have to travel.

We should read even Delille's pending beatification case through this eschatological lens. As Copeland recognizes, although Delille was a free woman of color who entered into a celibate union with God partially in order to escape a life spent as a white man's sexual prize, Delille's perceived nonwhiteness did not necessarily make her an enemy of antiblackness.[45] As in other former French colonies, such as Haiti, Louisiana's free people of color did not generally adopt a stance of solidarity with enslaved black people. Nor did they typically believe themselves to be members of a common race. Even as free people of color were victimized by white supremacy, they often helped to uphold black slavery.[46] For this reason, we should be careful not to overly romanticize Delille by assuming that she necessarily opposed or was even made uncomfortable by black slavery.

The church holds the past captive so as to avoid confessing itself as a master. Fugitive memories, like fugitive people, sever the church's hagiographical alliance with antiblackness supremacy for the way it reverses slavery's currents of debt and dependence. White people's collective habituation by antiblackness supremacy makes it difficult for us to let go of both black people and blackness completely and on our own. Black fugitivity does for white people what we cannot do for ourselves. Black fugitivity reconditions racially vicious wills by diminishing nonblack people's power to keep black people in the place of their choosing. It imposes on nonblack people a new reality to which they must become accustomed. As a hagiographical principle, fugitivity brings our parasitic dependence on both black people and blackness to light. Putting formerly captive memories out of our control, black fugitivity deprives us of the sense of honor these memories would have provided us.

Black fugitivity will not re-habituate the church all at once. The church can learn to love black fugitivity only over time and through

45. Copeland, *Subversive Power of Love*, 4, 11.
46. Sybil Kein, *Creole: The History and Legacy of Louisiana's Free People of Color* (Baton Rouge: Louisiana State University Press, 2000), 59–60, 257; Dubois, *Avengers of the New World*, 67, 166.

repeated practice. Like all moral agents, the church can begin to shed its vices only by acting against the grain of their conditioning. Just as a person ameliorates the vice of impoliteness, for example, simply by practicing politeness, so the church can begin to overcome its racial vices by admitting the existence of black ecclesial fugitives. The ends are the means: the church will have acquired racial virtue when it can acclaim black fugitivity as holy just as learning to acclaim black fugitivity as holy will help the church to acquire racial virtue. In matters of habit, one becomes what one does. None of the strategies proposed above can re-habituate the church on its own; but each one can carve out a little more space in which new racial habits can grow.

Conclusion

The vice of antiblackness supremacy and the vice of nostalgic unknowing empower one another. The church's desire to exonerate itself prevents it from acknowledging its racial vices while the uninterrupted operation of the church's racial vices encourages the church to believe itself worthy of exoneration. These vices operate within us despite our best intentions, revealing our best intentions to be less than good. Bearing bad racial habits, even the most racially progressive white Catholics have struggled to affirm in the concrete what they claim to desire in the abstract. We define racism as anything but our own mastership. Culpably ignorant of racial evil's true identity, we retain our racialized power without ceding our sense of moral righteousness. Like La Farge, Markoe, and Slattery, nonblack Catholics sometimes perpetuate antiblackness supremacy precisely by attempting to eliminate it.

So far, Catholic processes of saint making have generally attempted to pacify black people, portraying loyalty to the church as not just black people's moral duty but also their sole path to salvation. This framework has often cast captivity as God's will for Africanized people. Against this, fugitivity helps to detect, interrupt, and overturn hagiographical narratives spun in the shape of antiblackness supremacy. It does so in three ways: first, as a diagnostic tool, it improves the church's definition of racial evil and enhances its sense of moral culpability in it; second, as a principle of hagiographical interpretation, black fugitivity forces the church to accept its hagiographical fugitives without seeking to re-capture them; and third, as an actual historical practice, it imposes a more virtuous mode of existence upon an otherwise intransigent church. Like all moral agents, the church can re-habituate itself only so far; it must also be reconditioned by forces outside of itself.

Black fugitivity further overturns slavery's afterlife because it offers nonblack Catholics the salvation we need but do not deserve. It strips us of the vices we cannot relinquish on our own; it deprives us of power, delusions of goodness, and the ability to calibrate our proximity to black people. It points to a holy outside but cautions us that we cannot access this space without destroying it. It presents us with a new moral goal; rather than striving to be saviors of black people, nonblack Catholics, like the church itself, should instead help to facilitate their escape from anything that they believe holds them captive. Rather than either imposing community on black people or expecting intimacy with them, black fugitivity counsels nonblack people to make themselves worthy of an invitation from black people. It further conditions them to accept that such an invitation may never arrive, instructing nonblack people to abandon even the slightest sense of entitlement in relation to black people. The church needs its fugitives precisely because they do not need the church.

Bibliography

Abston, Emanuel J. "Catholicism and African Americans: A Study of Claverism, 1909–1959." PhD diss., Florida State University, 1998.

Alfani, Guido, and Vincent Gourdon. *Spiritual Kinship in Europe, 1500–1900.* Houndmills, Basingstoke, Eng.: Palgrave Macmillan, 2012.

Ali, Omar H. "The African Diaspora in Latin America: Afro-Peru and San Martín de Porres." *New African Review* 2, no. 4 (Summer 2013): 1–4.

Alim, H. Samy, and Angela Reyes. Introduction to "Complicating Race: Articulating Race across Multiple Social Dimensions." Special issue, *Discourse and Society* 22, no. 4 (July 1, 2011).

_____, and Geneva Smitherman. *Articulate while Black: Barack Obama, Language, and Race in the U.S.* Oxford: Oxford University Press, 2012.

Aquinas, Thomas. *Summa Theologica.* Translated by Fathers of the Dominican Province. New York: Benzinger Brothers, 1922.

Arana, Paola Vargas. "Pedro Claver y la evangelización en Cartagena: Pilar del encuentro entre africanos y el Nuevo Mundo, siglo XVII." *Fronteras de la historia* 11 (2006): 293–330.

Baptist, Edward E. *The Half Has Never Been Told: Slavery and the Making of American Capitalism.* Philadelphia: Basic Books, 2014.

Bassett, Molly H., and Vincent W. Lloyd, eds. *Sainthood and Race: Marked Flesh, Holy Flesh.* New York: Routledge, 2014.

Beattie, Tina. *New Catholic Feminism: Theology and Theory.* New York: Routledge, 2006.

Best, Stephen, and Saidiya Hartman. "Fugitive Justice." *Representations* 92, no. 1 (Fall 2005).

Birmingham, William. *Cross Currents: Exploring the Implications of Christianity for Our Times.* New York: Crossroad, 1989.

Block, Kristen. "Faith and Fortune: Religious Identity and the Politics of Profit in the Seventeenth-Century Caribbean." PhD diss., Rutgers University, 2007.

———. *Ordinary Lives in the Early Caribbean: Religion, Colonial Competition, and the Politics of Profit.* Athens: University of Georgia Press, 2012.

Blumenthal, Debra. *Enemies and Familiars: Slavery and Mastery in Fifteenth-Century Valencia.* Ithaca, NY: Cornell University Press, 2009.

Bogues, Anthony. "The Political Thought of Quobna Cugoano: Radicalized Natural Liberty." In *Black Heretics, Black Prophets: Radical Political Intellectuals.* New York: Routledge, 2003.

Borja, Jaime Humberto. "Cuerpo y mortificación en la hagiografía colonial neogranadina." *Theologica Xaveriana* 57, no. 162 (2007): 262–65. http://tinyurl.com/hvma3kx.

Brewer-García, Larissa. "Negro, pero blanco de alma: La ambivalencia de la negrura en la Vida prodigiosas de Fray Martín de Porras, 1663." *CILHA* 13, no. 17 (2012): 112–45.

Brioschi, Pedro A. *Vida de San Pedro Claver: Heroico apóstol de los negros.* Paris: Garnier Hermanos, 1889.

Canizares-Esguerra, Jorge, Matt D. Childs, and James Sidbury. *The Black Urban Atlantic in the Age of the Slave Trade.* Philadelphia: University of Pennsylvania Press, 2013.

Cannon, Katie Geneva. *Katie's Canon: Womanism and the Soul of the Black Community.* London: Bloomsbury Academic, 1998.

Carter, J. Kameron. *Race: A Theological Account.* Oxford: Oxford University Press, 2008.

Catechism of the Catholic Church. 2nd ed. Washington, DC: U.S. Catholic Conference, 2000.

Certeau, Michel de. *The Writing of History.* New York: Columbia University Press, 1988.

Chait, Jonathan. "Why Limbaugh Can't Stop Talking about Slavery." *New York,* October 6, 2014. http://tinyurl.com/zlkn2h2.

Chuavet, Louis-Marie. *The Sacraments—The Word of God at the Mercy of the Body.* Collegeville, MN: Liturgical Press, 2001.

_____. *Symbol and Sacrament: A Sacramental Reinterpretation of Christian Existence.* Collegeville, MN: Liturgical Press, 1995.

Colás, Yago. "A Desire Named Steph Curry." Between the Lines, June 16, 2015. http://tinyurl.com/zl88z4q.

Coleman, Monica A. *Making a Way Out of No Way: A Womanist Theology.* Minneapolis: Fortress Press, 2008.

Cone, James H. *God of the Oppressed.* 2nd ed. Maryknoll, NY: Orbis, 1997.

Cooper, William M. *The History of the Rod: Flagellation and the Flagellants from All Countries from the Earliest Period to the Present Time.* New York: Routledge, 2009.

Copeland, M. Shawn. "A Cadre of Women Religious Committed to Black Liberation: The National Black Sisters' Conference." *U.S. Catholic Historian* 14, no. 1 (1996): 123–44.

_____. *Enfleshing Freedom: Body, Race, and Being.* Minneapolis: Fortress Press, 2009.

_____. "The New Anthropological Subject at the Heart of the Mystical Body of Christ." *Proceedings of the Catholic Theological Society of America* 53 (2013).

_____. *The Subversive Power of Love: The Vision of Henriette Delille.* New York: Paulist Press, 2008.

Copeland, M. Shawn, ed., with LaReine-Marie Mosely and Albert J. Raboteau. *Uncommon Faithfulness: The Black Catholic Experience.* Maryknoll, NY: Orbis, 2009.

Cugoana, Ottabah. *Thoughts and Sentiments on the Evil and Wicked Traffic of the Slavery and Commerce of the Human Species, Humbly Submitted to the Inhabitants of Great-Britain, by Ottobah Cugoano.* London, 1787.

Cunningham, Lawrence S. "Saints and Martyrs: Some Contemporary Considerations." *Theological Studies* 60, no. 3 (1999): 529–30.

Cusack, Mary Francis. *The Black Pope: A History of the Jesuits.* London: Marshall, Russell, 1896.

Cussen, Celia Langdeau. *Black Saint of the Americas: The Life and Afterlife of Martín de Porres.* New York: Cambridge University Press, 2014.

_____. "Fray Martín de Porres and the Religious Imagination of Creole Lima." PhD diss., University of Pennsylvania, 1996.

David, Saul. "Slavery and the 'Scramble for Africa.'" BBC History, February 17, 2011. http://tinyurl.com/9hpg2oc.

Davis, Angela Y. *Abolition Democracy: Beyond Prison, Torture, and Empire.* New York: Seven Stories, 2005.

Davis, Cyprian. "The Holy See and American Black Catholics: A Forgotten Chapter in the History of the American Church." *U.S. Catholic Historian* 7, nos. 2–3 (1988): 157–81.

Davis, David Brion. *The Problem of Slavery in Western Culture.* New York: Oxford University Press, 1988.

Delehaye, Hippolyte. *The Legends of the Saints: An Introduction to Hagiography.* London: Longmans, Green, 1907.

Dionne, E. J., Jr. "Pope Apologizes to Africans for Slavery." *New York Times,* August 14, 1985.

Douglas, Kelly Brown. *Stand Your Ground: Black Bodies and the Justice of God.* Maryknoll, NY: Orbis, 2015.

Douglass, Frederick, and William Lloyd Garrison. *Narrative of the Life of Frederick Douglass, An American Slave.* Boston: The Anti-Slavery Office, 1849.

DuBois, Laurent. *Avengers of the New World: The Story of the Haitian Revolution.* Cambridge, MA: Harvard University Press, 2009.

Edelman, Ezra. *O. J.: Made in America* (film series). ESPN.com. Accessed December 5, 2016. http://tinyurl.com/z44je26.

Ellis, Robert Richmond. "Reading through the Veil of Juan Francisco Manzano: From Homoerotic Violence to the Dream of a Homoracial Bond." *PMLA* 113, no. 3 (May 1, 1998): 422–35.

Farley, Anthony P. "The Apogee of the Commodity." *DePaul Law Review* 53, (2004): 1229.

Farrelly, Maura Jane. "American Slavery, American Freedom, American Catholicism." *Early American Studies: An Interdisciplinary Journal* 10, no. 1 (2012).

Fink, John F. *American Saints: Five Centuries of Heroic Sanctity on the American Continents.* New York: Alba House, 2001.

Finotti, Joseph M. *Peter Claver: A Sketch of His Life and Labors in Behalf of the African Slave.* Boston: Lee & Shephard, 1868.

Fleuriau, Bertrand Gabriel. *The Life of the Venerable Father Claver, S.J., Apostle of the West Indies; and Memoirs of the Religious Life of Cardinal Odescalchi, S.J.* London: Richardson, 1849.

Franklin, Vincent P. "Bibliographical Essay: Alonso De Sandoval and the Jesuit Conception of the Negro." *Journal of Negro History* 58, no. 3 (July 1, 1973).

Garces, Chris. "The Interspecies Logic of Race in Colonial Peru: San Martín de Porres's Animal Brotherhood." In *Sainthood and Race: Marked Flesh, Holy Flesh.* Edited by Molly H. Bassett and Vincent W. Lloyd. New York: Routledge, 2014.

García-Rivera, Alejandro. "St. Martin de Porres: Emblem of a Latin American Anthropology." PhD diss., Lutheran School of Theology at Chicago, 1994.

_____. *St. Martín de Porres: The "Little Stories" and the Semiotics of Culture.* Maryknoll, NY: Orbis, 1995.

George, Francis. *Dwell in My Love: A Pastoral Letter on Racism,* April 4, 2001. http://tinyurl.com/jkwhgbk.

Georges, Norbert. *With Blessed Martin De Porres: Favorite Stories from The Torch* New York: Blessed Martin Guild, 1944.

Germeten, Nicole von. "A Century of Promoting Saint Peter Claver and Catholicism to African Americans: Claverian Historiography from 1868–1965." *American Catholic Studies* 116, no. 3 (2005): 23–38.

_____. "The Problems and Challenges of Research and Writing on Africans and their Descendants in Colonial Cartagena de Indies: A Research Report." Center for Africana Studies Working Paper Series, no. 002, Johns Hopkins University. http://tinyurl.com/zx4t4mq.

Glissant, Édouard. *Caribbean Discourse: Selected Essays.* Charlottesville: University Press of Virginia, 1989.

Golash-Boza, Tanya Maria. *Yo Soy Negro: Blackness in Peru.* Gainesville: University Press of Florida, 2011.

Goldberg, Jonah. "Oprah, Obama, and the Racism Dodge." *National Review Online,* November 20, 2013. http://tinyurl.com/pulet76.

Gómez Zuluaga, Pablo Fernando. "Bodies of Encounter: Health, Illness, and

Death in the Early Modern African-Spanish Caribbean." PhD diss., Vanderbilt University, 2010.

González, Ondina E., and Justo L. González. *Christianity in Latin America: A History.* New York: Cambridge University Press, 2008.

Greggus, David Patrick. *The World of the Haitian Revolution.* Bloomington: Indiana University Press, 2009.

Griffin, Beth. "Black History Month Opens with Mass at St. Patrick's Cathedral." *National Catholic Reporter,* February 3, 2015. http://tinyurl.com/hjqqnl3.

Grimes, Katie M. "Black Exceptionalism: Antiblackness Supremacy and the Afterlife of Slavery." In Vincent Lloyd and Andrew Prevot, *Antiblackness and Christian Ethics.* Maryknoll, NY: Orbis, *forthcoming.*

_____. "Breaking the Body of Christ: The Sacraments of Initiation in a Habitat of White Supremacy." *Political Theology* (forthcoming).

Guelzo, Allen C. "Should Blacks Get Reparations?" *Christian Science Monitor,* July 16, 2009. http://tinyurl.com/homd5nv.

Hanley, Boniface. *Ten Christians: By Their Deeds You Shall Know Them.* Notre Dame, IN: Ave Maria Press, 1979.

Harms, Robert. *The Diligent: A Voyage through the Worlds of the Slave Trade.* New York: Basic Books, 2002.

Hartman, Saidiya V. *Lose Your Mother: A Journey Along the Atlantic Slave Route.* New York: Farrar, Straus & Giroux, 2008.

_____. *Scenes of Subjection: Terror, Slavery, and Self-Making in Nineteenth Century America.* New York: Oxford University Press, 1997.

Hinze, Bradford E. "Ecclesial Repentance and the Demands of Dialogue." *Theological Studies* 61, no. 2 (June 20): 207–38.

Home, Gerald. *Confronting Black Jacobins: The U.S., the Haitian Revolution, and the Dominican Republic.* New York: New York University Press, 2015.

Jackson, R. "Plaque Honors 18th Century New York Man." *Indianapolis Recorder,* July 21, 1951.

Jennings, Willie James. *The Christian Imagination: Theology and the Origins of Race.* New Haven, CT: Yale University Press, 2010.

Johnson, Elizabeth A. *Friends of God and Prophets: A Feminist Theological Reading of the Communion of Saints.* New York: Continuum, 1998.

Johnson, Karen J. "The Universal Church in the Segregated City: Doing Catholic

Interracialism in Chicago, 1915–1963." PhD diss., University of Illinois, Chicago, 2013.

Johnson, Sylvester. "The African American Christian Tradition." In *The Oxford Handbook of African American Theology*. Edited by Katie G. Cannon and Anthony B. Pinn. New York: Oxford University Press, 2014.

Jones-Armstrong, Amaryah. "Blackness and Value, Part 2: On Whiteness as Credit." *Women in Theology* (February 11, 2015). http://tinyurl.com/zp6zgtn.

_____. "On the Theo-political Vision of Macklemore; or, Why Proximity & Intimacy ≠ Solidarity." *Women in Theology* (June 16, 2013). http://tinyurl.com/j3g89b5.

Jones, Arthur. *Pierre Toussaint*. New York: Random House, 2003.

Joseph, Mark. "No, Oprah, America Isn't Racist." *USA TODAY*, November 24, 2013. http://tinyurl.com/zu7vfr7.

Kein, Sybil. *Creole: The History and Legacy of Louisiana's Free People of Color*. Baton Rouge, LA: Louisiana State University Press, 2000.

Kelley, Robin D.G. *Freedom Dreams: The Black Radical Imagination*. Boston: Beacon, 2002.

King, James Ferguson. "Descriptive Data on Negro Slaves in Spanish Importation Records and Bills of Sale." *The Journal of Negro History* 28, no. 2 (Apr 1943): 204–19.

Klein, Martin A. *Historical Dictionary of Slavery and Abolition*. 2nd ed. Lanham, MD: Rowman & Littlefield, 2014.

La Farge, John. "The Humility of Martin de Porres." *Interracial Review* 35 (September 1962).

_____. *The Race Question and the Negro: A Study of the Catholic Doctrine on Interracial Justice*. New York: Longmans, Green, 1937.

LaFraniere, Sharon, and Mitch Smith. "Philando Castile Was Pulled Over 49 Times in 13 Years, Often for Minor Infractions." *New York Times*, July 16, 2016. http://tinyurl.com/j4xod7g.

Landers, Jane. "Founding Mothers: Female Rebels in Colonial New Granada and Spanish Florida." *Journal of African American History* 98, no. 1 (2013).

_____. "La Cultura Material De Los Cimarrones: Los Casos De Ecuador, La Española, México Y Colombia," in *Rutas De La Esclavitud En África Y América*

Latina San José, edited by Rina Cáceres. Costa Rica: Editorial de la Universidad de Costa Rica, 2001.

Lee, Hannah Farnham Sawyer. *Memoir of Pierre Toussaint, Born a Slave in St. Domingo.* Boston: Crosby, Nichols, Lee, 1854.

Leo XIII. *In Plurimis: Encyclical of Pope Leo XIII on the Abolition of Slavery.* 1888. http://tinyurl.com/zapmb5c.

Lott, Eric. *Love and Theft: Blackface Minstrelsy and the American Working Class.* New York: Oxford University Press, 1993.

Markoe, William Morgan. *The Slave of the Negroes.* Chicago: Loyola University Press, 1920.

Martin, James. *The Jesuit Guide to (Almost) Everything: A Spirituality for Real Life.* New York: HarperCollins, 2010.

Massingale, Bryan N. *Racial Justice and the Catholic Church.* Maryknoll, NY: Orbis, 2010.

———. "*Vox Victimarum Vox Dei:* Malcolm X as Neglected 'Classic' for Catholic Theological Reflection." *CTSA Proceedings* 65 (2010).

McCarthy, Justin. *Pope Leo XIII. Public Men of To-Day.* New York: Frederick Warne, 1896.

McGreevy, John T. *Catholicism and American Freedom: A History.* New York: Norton, 2003.

———. *Parish Boundaries: The Catholic Encounter with Race in the Twentieth-Century Urban North.* Chicago: University of Chicago Press, 1998.

McKnight, Kathryn Joy. "Elder, Slave and Solider: Maroon Voices from the Palenque del Limón, 1634." In *Afro-Latino Voices,* edited by Kathryn Joy McKnight and Leo J. Garofalo. Indianapolis: Hackett, 2009.

McLean, Candace. "'Do This In Memory of Me': The Genealogy and Theological Appropriations of Memory in the Work of Johann Baptist Metz." PhD diss., University of Notre Dame, 2012.

McWhirter, Cameron. *Red Summer: The Summer of 1919 and the Awakening of Black America.* New York: Henry Holt, 2011.

Medina, Bernardo de. *Vida prodigiosa del venerable siervo de Dios Fr. Martin de Porras.* Madrid: Domingo Garcia Morrás, 1675.

Mikulich, Alex, Laurie Cassidy, and Margaret Pfeil. *The Scandal of White*

Complicity in U.S. Hyper-incarceration: A Nonviolent Spirituality of White Resistance. New York: Palgrave Macmillan, 2013.

Mintz, Sidney W., and Eric R. Wolf. "An Analysis of Ritual Co-parenthood (Compadrazgo)." *Southwestern Journal of Anthropology* 6, no. 4 (December 1, 1950).

Moitt, Bernard. *Women and Slavery in the French Antilles, 1635–1848.* Bloomington: Indiana University Press, 2001.

Moore, Cecilia A. "Victor and Constance Daniel and Emancipatory Education at the Cardinal Gibbons Institute." *Journal of Catholic Education* 4, no. 3 (2001).

Mosely, LaReine-Marie. "Daniel A. Rudd and His *American Catholic Tribune*: Faithful and Prophetic in Passing On the Tradition." In *Uncommon Faithfulness: The Black Catholic Experience*, edited by M. Shawn Copeland. Maryknoll, NY: Orbis, 2009.

Moten, Fred. "Blackness and Nothingness (Mysticism in the Flesh)." *South Atlantic Quarterly* 112, no. 4 (2013): 737–80.

_____. "The Case of Blackness." *Criticism* 50, no. 2 (2008).

Neely, Alan. "Saints Who Sometimes Were: Utilizing Missionary Hagiography." *Missiology: An International Review* 27, no. 4 (October 1, 1999).

Newsom, Linda A. *From Capture to Sale: The Portuguese Slave Trade to Spanish South America in the Early Seventeenth Century.* Leiden: Brill, 2007.

Noonan, John T. *A Church That Can and Cannot Change: The Development of Catholic Moral Teaching.* Notre Dame, IN: University of Notre Dame Press, 2005.

O'Connor, John. "In the Cathedral Crypt, a Prayer for Haiti." *Catholic New York,* October 21, 1993. http://tinyurl.com/znx3erz.

O'Donovan, Leo J. "A Changing Ecclesiology in a Changing Church: A Symposium on Development in the Ecclesiology of Karl Rahner." *Theological Studies* 38, no. 4 (1977): 736.

"O'Reilly Clashes with Harvard Professor over Oprah: She's 'Indicting' America as a Racist Nation," FoxNation.com, November 19, 2013. http://tinyurl.com/zy4x943.

Palacios, Marcos, and Frank Safford. *Colombia: País fragmentado, sociedad dividida. Su historia.* Bogotá, Colombia: Grupo Editorial Norma, 2005.

Patterson, Orlando. *Slavery and Social Death: A Comparative Study.* Cambridge, MA: Harvard University Press, 1985.

Paul VI. *Dogmatic Constitution on the Church—Lumen Gentium.* Vatican: Holy See, 1965.

Penyak, Lee Michael. "Criminal Sexuality in Central Mexico, 1750–1850." PhD diss., University of Connecticut, 1993.

Petre, Maude Dominica Mary. *Aethiopum Servus: A Study in Christian Altruism.* London: Osgood, McIlvaine, 1896; repr., Memphis, TN: General Books, 2010.

Portier, William L. "John R. Slattery's Vision for the Evangelization of American Blacks." *U.S. Catholic Historian* 5, no. 1 (1986): 19–44.

Powers, Karen Vieira. *Women in the Crucible of Conquest: The Gendered Genesis of Spanish American Society, 1500-1600.* Albuquerque: University of New Mexico Press, 2005.

Preher, Leo Marie. *The Social Implications in the Work of Blessed Martin de Porres.* Washington, DC: Catholic University of America Press, 1941.

Prien, Hans-Jürgen. *Christianity in Latin America.* Leiden: Brill, 2012.

Prusak, Bernard P. "Theological Considerations—Hermeneutical, Ecclesiological, and Eschatological Regarding *Memory and Reconciliation: The Church and the Faults of the Past,*" *Horizons* 32, no. 1 (April 2005): 136–51.

Raboteau, Albert J. "Relating Race and Religion: Four Historical Models." In *Uncommon Faithfulness: The Black Catholic Experience,* edited by M. Shawn Copeland. Maryknoll, NY: Orbis, 2009.

Rahner, Karl. "Observations on the Problem of the 'Anonymous' Christian." *Theological Investigations* 14 (1976): 280–94.

_____, and William F. Gleeson. "The Church of Sinners." *CrossCurrents* 1, no. 3 (1951): 64–74.

Redden, Andrew. "The Problem of Witchcraft, Slavery, and Jesuits in Seventeenth-Century New Granada." *Bulletin of Hispanic Studies* 90, no. 2 (2013).

Rediker, Marcus. *The Slave Ship: A Human History.* New York: Penguin, 2008.

Rice, Lincoln R. "Confronting the Heresy of 'The Mythical Body of Christ': The Life of Dr. Arthur Falls." *American Catholic Studies* 123, no. 2 (2012).

Rivera, Luis N. *A Violent Evangelism: The Political and Religious Conquest of the Americas.* Louisville, KY: Westminster John Knox, 1992.

Roberts, Neil. *Freedom as Marronage: The Dialectic of Slavery and Freedom in Arendt,*

Pettit, Rousseau, Douglass, and the Haitian Revolution. PhD diss., The University of Chicago, 2007.

Rodriguez, Junius P. *Encyclopedia of Slave Resistance and Rebellion.* Vol. 2. Westport, CT: Greenwood, 2007.

Sanchez, Maria Carla. *Reforming the World: Social Activism and the Problem of Fiction in Nineteenth Century America.* Iowa City: University of Iowa Press, 2009.

Sanders, Katrina M. "Black Catholic Clergy and the Struggle for Civil Rights." In *Uncommon Faithfulness: The Black Catholic Experience,* edited by M. Shawn Copeland. Maryknoll, NY: Orbis, 2009.

Sandoval, Alonso de. *Treatise on Slavery: Selections from "De instauranda Aethiopum salute."* Edited and translated by Nicole von Germeten. Indianapolis: Hackett, 2007.

Scheid, Anna Floerke. *Just Revolution: A Christian Ethic of Political Resistance and Social Transformation.* Lanham, MD: Lexington, 2015.

Schiller, Nina Glick, and Georges Eugene Fouron. "'The Blood Remains Haitian': Race, Nation, and Belonging in the Transmigrant Experience." In Philip W. Scher, *Perspectives on the Caribbean: A Reader in Culture, History, and Representation.* West Sussex, UK: John Wiley & Sons, 2010.

Schorr, Daniel. "A New, 'Post-Racial' Political Era in America." NPR.org, January 28, 2008. http://tinyurl.com/mypcmr.

Schorsch, Jonathan. *Jews and Blacks in the Early Modern World.* Cambridge: Cambridge University Press, 2004.

Schroth, Raymond A. *The American Jesuits: A History.* New York: New York University Press, 2007.

Schuster, Ekkehard, and Reinhold Boschert-Kimmig. *Hope against Hope: Johann Baptist Metz and Elie Wiesel Speak Out on the Holocaust.* Translated by J. Matthew Ashley. New York: Paulist Press, 1999.

Scott, James C. *Domination and the Arts of Resistance: Hidden Transcripts.* New Haven, CT: Yale University Press, 1990.

Second Vatican Council. *Constitution on the Church = Lumen Gentium.* Washington, DC: National Catholic Welfare Conference, 1964.

Sexton, Jared. "Afro-pessimism: The Unclear Word." *Rhizomes: Cultural Studies in Emerging Knowledge,* no. 29 (2016). http://tinyurl.com/joxt76z.

_____. *Amalgamation Schemes: Antiblackness and the Critique of Multiculturalism.* Minneapolis: University of Minnesota Press, 2008.

_____. "People-of-Color-Blindness: Notes on the Afterlife of Slavery." *Social Text* 28, no. 2 (June 20, 2010).

_____. "The Social Life of Social Death: On Afro-pessimism and Black Optimism." *Tensions*, no. 5 (Fall–Winter 2011).

Skocpol, Theda, and Jennifer Lynn Oser. "Organization despite Adversity: The Origins and Development of African American Fraternal Organizations." *Social Science History* 28 (2004).

Slattery, John Richard. *The Life of St. Peter Claver, S.J.: The Apostle of the Negroes.* Philadelphia: Kilner, 1893.

Spillers, Hortense J. "Mama's Baby, Papa's Maybe: An American Grammar Book." In *Black, White, and in Color: Essays on American Literature and Culture.* Chicago: University of Chicago Press, 2003.

Sobrino, Jon. *Jesus the Liberator: A Historical-Theological Reading of Jesus of Nazareth.* Translated by Paul Burns and Francis McDonagh. Maryknoll, NY: Orbis, 1994.

Sontag, Deborah. "Canonizing a Slave: Saint or Uncle Tom?" *New York Times,* February 23, 1992.

Southern, David W. *John LaFarge and the Limits of Catholic Interracialism, 1911–1963.* Baton Rouge: Louisiana State University Press, 1996.

Splendiani, Anna María. "Un jesuita y una cuidad: Pedro Claver y Cartagena de Indias," t.l, mecanografiado. Bogotá: Colciencias, 2000.

_____, and Tulio Aristizábal. *El proceso de beatificación y canonización de San Pedro Claver.* Bogotá: Pontificia Universidad Javeriana, 2002.

Splendiani, Anna María, José Enrique Sánchez Bohórquez, and Emma Cecilia Luque de Salazar. *Cincuenta años de Inquisición en el Tribunal de Cartagena de Indias, 1610–1660: Documentos inéditos procedentes del Archivo Histórico Nacional de Madrid (AHNM), libro 1020, años 1610–1637.* Vol. 2. Bogotá: Centro editorial Javeriano, Instituto colombiano de cultura hispánica, 1997.

Sullivan, Francis A. "Catholic Tradition and Traditions." In *The Crisis of Authority in Catholic Modernity*, edited by Michael J. Lacey and Francis Oakley. Oxford: Oxford University Press, 2011.

_____. *Salvation Outside the Church?: Tracing the History of the Catholic Response.* Eugene, OR: Wipf and Stock, 1992.

Sweet, David G. "'Black Robes and 'Black Destiny': Jesuit Views of African Slavery in 17th-Century Latin America." *Revista de Historia de América* 86 (1978).

Sweet, James H. "Collective Degradation: Slavery and the Construction of Race." *America* 1492 (2003).

Tarry, Ellen. *The Other Toussaint: A Post-Revolutionary Black.* Boston: Daughters of St. Paul, 1981.

Taylor, Eric Robert. *If We Must Die: Shipboard Insurrections in the Era of the Atlantic Slave Trade.* Baton Rouge: Louisiana State University Press, 2006.

Tentler, Thomas N. *Sin and Confession on the Eve of the Reformation.* Princeton, NJ: Princeton University Press, 1977.

Thomas, Hugh. *The Slave Trade: The Story of the Atlantic Trade, 1440–1870.* New York: Simon & Schuster Paperbacks, 1997.

Tinker, George E. *Missionary Conquest: The Gospel and Native American Cultural Genocide.* Minneapolis: Fortress Press, 1993.

Tortorici, Zeb Joseph. "Contra Natura: Sin, Crime, and 'Unnatural' Sexuality in Colonial Mexico, 1530–1821." PhD diss., University of California, Los Angeles, 2010.

T'Serclaes de Wommersom, Charles de. *The Life and Labors of Pope Leo XIII: With a Summary of His Important Letters, Addresses, and Encyclicals.* Chicago: Rand, McNally, 1903.

United States Conference of Catholic Bishops. "The Corporal Works of Mercy." USCCB.org, New Evangelization. Accessed July 28, 2016. http://tinyurl.com/jry25xf.

Valtierra, Angel. *Peter Claver: Saint of the Slaves.* Westminster, MD: Newman, 1960.

Vogt, Brandon. *Saints and Social Justice: A Guide to Changing the World.* Huntington, IN: Our Sunday Visitor, 2014.

Wade, Peter. *Blackness and Race Mixture: The Dynamics of Racial Identity in Colombia.* Baltimore: Johns Hopkins University Press, 1995.

Ward, Haruko Nawata. *Women Religious Leaders in Japan's Christian Century, 1549-1650.* Burlington, VT: Ashgate, 2009.

West, Traci. "When a White Man-God Is the Truth and the Way for Black Christians." In *Christology and Whiteness: What Would Jesus Do?*, edited by George Yancy. New York: Routledge, 2012.

White, Ashli. *Encountering Revolution: Haiti and the Making of the Early Republic.* Baltimore: Johns Hopkins University Press, 2010.

White, Owen. *In God's Empire: French Missionaries in the Modern World.* New York: Oxford University Press, 2012.

Wilderson, Frank B., III. *Red, White, and Black: Cinema and the Structure of U.S. Antagonisms.* Durham, NC: Duke University Press, 2010.

Wreck, D. "Pat Buchanan: Slavery Best Thing Ever to Happen to Blacks." *Daily Kos*, March 22, 2008. http://tinyurl.com/zcb9uk3.

Yancy, George, ed. *Christology and Whiteness: What Would Jesus Do?* New York: Routledge, 2012.

Index